GOD'S WISDOM
for Business Success

GOD'S WISDOM
for Business Success

WORD PUBLISHING
Dallas•London•Vancouver•Melbourne

GOD'S WISDOM FOR BUSINESS SUCCESS

Unless otherwise noted, Scripture quotations are from
The Holy Bible, King James Version.

Library of Congress Cataloging-in-Publication Data

God's wisdom for business success.
     p.   cm.
ISBN: 978-1-4041-7557-0
1. Business—Biblical teaching.   2. Business—Religious
aspects—Christianity.   3. Bible—Use.   I. Word Publishing.
BS680.B8G63   1995
248.8'8—dc20   95-11752
                                       CIP

Printed in Belgium

Contents

Contents

5. Biblical Ethics For Your Business • 147

6. Biblical Standards With Business Associates • 179

7. Biblical Counsel For Trying Times In Your Business • 225

8. Biblical Strengths For Your Business Success • 265

Biblical Basics To Begin Your Business...

Vision & Purpose

Let thine eyes look right on, and let thine eyelids look straight before thee.

Ponder the path of thy feet, and let all thy ways be established.

Turn not to the right hand nor to the left: remove thy foot from evil.

Proverbs 4:25-27

Where (there is) no vision, the people perish: but he that keepeth the law, happy (is) he.

Proverbs 29:18

I therefore, the prisoner of the Lord, beseech you that ye walk worthy of the vocation wherewith ye are called,

With all lowliness and meekness, with long-suffering, forbearing one another in love;

Endeavouring to keep the unity of the Spirit in the bond of peace.

Ephesians 4:1-3

Brethren, I count not myself to have apprehended: but (this) one thing (I do), forgetting those things which are behind, and reaching forth unto those things which are before,

I press toward the mark for the prize of the high calling of God in Christ Jesus.

Philippians 3:13, 14

The simple believeth every word: but the prudent (man) looketh well to his going.

Proverbs 14:15

(Every) purpose is established by counsel: and with good advice make war.

Proverbs 20:18

Man's goings (are) of the LORD; how can a man then understand his own way?

Proverbs 20:24

Only be thou strong and very courageous, that thou mayest observe to do according to all the law, which Moses my servant commanded thee: turn not from it (to) the right hand or (to) the left, that thou mayest prosper whithersoever thou goest.

Joshua 1:7

Ye have not chosen me, but I have chosen you, and ordained you, that ye should go and bring forth fruit, and (that) your fruit should remain: that whatsoever ye shall ask of the Father in my name, he may give it you.

John 15:16

And Jesus came and spake unto them, saying, All power is given unto me in heaven and in earth.

Go ye therefore, and teach all nations, baptizing them in the name of the Father, and of the Son, and of the Holy Ghost:

Teaching them to observe all things what-soever I have commanded you: and, lo, I am with you alway, (even) unto the end of the world. Amen.

Matthew 28:18-20

A man's heart deviseth his way: but the Lord directeth his steps.

Proverbs 16:9

O Lord, I know that the way of man is not in himself: it is not in man that walketh to direct his steps.

Jeremiah 10:23

Trust in the Lord with all thine heart; and lean not unto thine own understanding.
In all thy ways acknowledge him, and he shall direct thy paths.

Proverbs 3:5, 6

But ye shall receive power, after that the Holy Ghost is come upon you: and ye shall be witnesses unto me both in Jerusalem, and in all Judaea, and in Samaria, and unto the uttermost part of the earth.

Acts 1:8

To every(thing there is) a season, and a time to every purpose under the heaven:

Ecclesiastes 3:1

I said in mine heart, God shall judge the righteous and the wicked: for (there is) a time there for every purpose and for every work.

Ecclesiastes 3:17

But rise, and stand upon thy feet: for I have appeared unto thee for this purpose, to make thee a minister and a witness both of these things which thou hast seen, and of those things in the which I will appear unto thee;

Acts 26:16

And we know that all things work together for good to them that love God, to them who are the called according to (his) purpose.

Romans 8:28

Wisdom & Guidance

The LORD by wisdom hath founded the earth; by understanding hath he established the heavens.

By his knowledge the depths are broken up, and the clouds drop down the dew.

My son, let not them depart from thine eyes: keep sound wisdom and discretion:

So shall they be life unto thy soul, and grace to thy neck.

Proverbs 3:19-22

Happy (is) the man (that) findeth wisdom, and the man (that) getteth understanding.

For the merchandise of it (is) better than the merchandise of silver, and the gain thereof than fine gold.

She (is) more precious than rubies: and all the things thou canst desire are not to be compared unto her.

Length of days (is) in her right hand; (and) in her left hand riches and honour.

Her ways (are) ways of pleasantness, and all her paths (are) peace.

Proverbs 3:13-17

Wisdom (is) good with an inheritance: and (by it there is) profit to them that see the sun.

For wisdom (is) a defence, (and) money (is) a defence: but the excellency of knowledge (is, that) wisdom giveth life to them that have it.

Ecclesiastes 7:11, 12

Wisdom (is) the principal thing; (therefore) get wisdom: and with all thy getting get understanding.

Exalt her, and she shall promote thee: she shall bring thee to honour, when thou dost embrace her.

Proverbs 4:7, 8

The fear of the LORD (is) the beginning of wisdom: and the knowledge of the holy (is) understanding.

Proverbs 9:10

For by wise counsel thou shalt make thy war: and in multitude of counsellors (there is) safety.
Proverbs 24:6

My son, eat thou honey, because (it is) good; and the honeycomb, (which is) sweet to thy taste:
So (shall) the knowledge of wisdom (be) unto thy soul: when thou hast found (it), then there shall be a reward, and thy expectation shall not be cut off.
Proverbs 24:13, 14

If any of you lack wisdom, let him ask of God, that giveth to all (men) liberally, and upbraideth not; and it shall be given him.
But let him ask in faith, nothing wavering. For he that wavereth is like a wave of the sea driven with the wind and tossed.

James 1:5, 6

And all Israel heard of the judgment which the king had judged; and they feared the king: for they saw that the wisdom of God (was) in him, to do judgment.

I Kings 3:28

And God gave Solomon wisdom and understanding exceeding much, and largeness of heart, even as the sand that (is) on the sea shore.

And Solomon's wisdom excelled the wisdom of all the children of the east country, and all the wisdom of Egypt.

I Kings 4:29, 30

Counsel (is) mine, and sound wisdom: I (am) understanding; I have strength.

Proverbs 8:14

This wisdom have I seen also under the sun, and it (seemed) great unto me:

(There was) a little city, and few men within it; and there came a great king against it, and besieged it, and built great bulwarks against it:

Now there was found in it a poor wise man, and he by his wisdom delivered the city; yet no man remembered that same poor man.

Then said I, Wisdom (is) better than strength: nevertheless the poor man's wisdom (is) despised, and his words are not heard.

The words of wise (men are) heard in quiet more than the cry of him that ruleth among fools.

Wisdom (is) better than weapons of war: but one sinner destroyeth much good.

Ecclesiates 9:13-18

Give me now wisdom and knowledge, that I may go out and come in before this people: for who can judge this thy people, (that is so) great?

And God said to Solomon, Because this was in thine heart, and thou hast not asked riches, wealth, or honour, nor the life of thine enemies, neither yet hast asked long life; but hast asked wisdom and knowledge for thyself, that thou mayest judge my people, over whom I have made thee king:

Wisdom and knowledge (is) granted unto thee; and I will give thee riches, and wealth, and honour, such as none of the kings have had that (have been) before thee, neither shall there any after thee have the like.

II Chronicles 1:10-12

So teach (us) to number our days, that we may apply (our) hearts unto wisdom.

Psalms 90:12

The fear of the LORD (is) the beginning of wisdom: a good understanding have all they that do (his commandments): his praise endureth for ever.

Psalms 111:10

My son, let not them depart from thine eyes: keep sound wisdom and discretion:

Proverbs 3:21

He that getteth wisdom loveth his own soul: he that keepeth understanding shall find good.

Proverbs 19:8

For this cause we also, since the day we heard (it), do not cease to pray for you, and to desire that ye might be filled with the knowledge of his will in all wisdom and spiritual understanding;

That ye might walk worthy of the Lord unto all pleasing, being fruitful in every good work, and increasing in the knowledge of God;

Strengthened with all might, according to his glorious power, unto all patience and longsuffering with joyfulness;

Colossians 1:9-11

Let the word of Christ dwell in you richly in all wisdom; teaching and admonishing one another in psalms and hymns and spiritual songs, singing with grace in your hearts to the Lord.

Colossians 3:16

Walk in wisdom toward them that are without, redeeming the time.

Colossians 4:5

The simple believeth every word: but the prudent (man) looketh well to his going.

A wise man feareth, and departeth from evil: but a fool rageth, and is confident.

Proverbs 14:15, 16

The heart of the prudent getteth knowledge; and the ear of the wise seeketh knowledge.

Proverbs 18:15

Creativity

In the beginning God created the heaven and the earth.

And the earth was without form, and void; and darkness (was) upon the face of the deep. And the Spirit of God moved upon the face of the waters.

Genesis 1:1, 2

And God said, Let us make man in our image, after our likeness: and let them have dominion over the fish of the sea, and over the fowl of the air, and over the cattle, and over all the earth, and over every creeping thing that creepeth upon the earth.

So God created man in his (own) image, in the image of God created he him, male and female created he them.

Genesis 1:26, 27

When I consider thy heavens, the work of thy fingers, the moon and the stars, which thou hast ordained;

What is man, that thou art mindful of him? and the son of man, that thou visitest him?

Psalms 8:3, 4

And, behold, men brought in a bed a man which was taken with a palsy: and they sought (means) to bring him in, and to lay (him) before him.

And when they could not find by what (way) they might bring him in because of the multitude, they went upon the housetop, and let him down through the tiling with (his) couch into the midst before Jesus.

And when he saw their faith, he said unto him, Man, thy sins are forgiven thee.

Luke 5:18-20

And there went a man of the house of Levi, and took (to wife) a daughter of Levi.

And the woman conceived, and bare a son: and when she saw him that he (was a) goodly (child), she hid him three months.

And when she could not longer hide him, she took for him an ark of bulrushes, and daubed it with slime and with pitch, and put the child therein; and she laid (it) in the flags by the river's brink.

And his sister stood afar off, to wit what would be done to him.

And the daughter of Pharaoh came down to wash (herself) at the river; and her maidens walked along by the river's side; and when she saw the ark among the flags, she sent her maid to fetch it.

And when she had opened (it), she saw the child: and, behold, the babe wept. And she had compassion on him, and said, This (is one) of the Hebrews' children.

Then said his sister to Pharaoh's daughter, Shall I go and call to thee a nurse of the Hebrew women, that she may nurse the child for thee?

And Pharaoh's daughter said to her, Go. And the maid went and called the child's mother.

And Pharaoh's daughter said unto her, Take this child away, and nurse it for me, and I will give (thee) thy wages. And the woman took the child, and nursed it.

And the child grew, and she brought him unto Pharaoh's daughter, and he became her son. And she called his name Moses: and she said, Because I drew him out of the water.

Exodus 2:1-10

Therefore if any man (be) in Christ, (he is) a new creature: old things are passed away; behold, all things are become new.

II Corinthians 5:17

And the LORD spake unto Moses, saying,

See, I have called by name Bezaleel the son of Uri, the son of Hur, of the tribe of Judah:

And I have filled him with the spirit of God, in wisdom, and in understanding, and in knowledge, and in all manner of workmanship,

To devise cunning works, to work in gold, and in silver, and in brass,

And in cutting of stones, to set (them), and in carving of timber, to work in all manner of workmanship.

Exodus 31:1-5

Wealth (gotten) by vanity shall be diminished: but he that gathereth by labour shall increase.

Proverbs 13:11

Them hath he filled with wisdom of heart, to work all manner of work, of the engraver, and of the cunning workman, and of the embroiderer, in blue, and in purple, in scarlet, and in fine linen, and of the weaver, (even) of them that do any work, and of those that devise cunning work.

Exodus 35:35

And Uzziah prepared for them throughout all the host shields, and spears, and helmets, and habergeons, and bows, and slings (to cast) stones.

And he made in Jerusalem engines, invented by cunning men, to be on the towers and upon the bulwarks, to shoot arrows and great stones withal. And his name spread far abroad; for he was marvellously helped, till he was strong.

II Chronicles 26:14, 15

Moreover (there are) workmen with thee in abundance, hewers and workers of stone and timber, and all manner of cunning men for every manner of work.

Of the gold, the silver, and the brass, and the iron, (there is) no number. Arise (therefore), and be doing, and the LORD be with thee.

Now set your heart and your soul to seek the LORD your God; arise therefore, and build ye the sanctuary of the LORD God, to bring the ark of the covenant of the LORD, and the holy vessels of God, into the house that is to be built to the name of the LORD.

I Chronicles 22:15, 16, 19

Ambition

Brethren, I count not myself to have apprehended: but (this) one thing (I do), forgetting those things which are behind, and reaching forth unto those things which are before,

I press toward the mark for the prize of the high calling of God in Christ Jesus.

Philippians 3:13, 14

And seek not ye what ye shall eat, or what ye shall drink, neither be ye of doubtful mind.

For all these things do the nations of the world seek after: and your Father knoweth that ye have need of these things.

But rather seek ye the kingdom of God; and all these things shall be added unto you.

Luke 12:29-31

Therefore, brethren, stand fast, and hold the traditions which ye have been taught, whether by word, or our epistle.

II Thessalonians 2:15

For what is a man profited, if he shall gain the whole world, and lose his own soul? or what shall a man give in exchange for his soul?

Matthew 16:26

Whatsoever thy hand findeth to do, do (it) with thy might; for (there is) no work, nor device, nor knowledge, nor wisdom, in the grave, whither thou goest.

Ecclesiastes 9:10

And James and John, the sons of Zebedee, come unto him, saying, Master, we would that thou shouldest do for us whatsoever we shall desire.

And he said unto them, What would ye that I should do for you?

They said unto him, Grant unto us that we may sit, one on thy right hand, and the other on thy left hand, in thy glory.

But Jesus said unto them, Ye know not what ye ask: can ye drink of the cup that I drink of? and be baptized with the baptism that I am baptized with?

And they said unto him, We can. And Jesus said unto them, Ye shall indeed drink of the cup that I drink of; and with the baptism that I am baptized withal shall ye be baptized:

But to sit on my right hand and on my left hand is not mine to give; but (it shall be given to them) for whom it is prepared.

And when the ten heard (it), they began to be much displeased with James and John.

But Jesus called them (to him), and saith unto them, Ye know that they which are accounted to rule over the Gentiles exercise lordship over them; and their great ones exercise authority upon them.

But so shall it not be among you: but whosoever will be great among you, shall be your minister:

And whosoever of you will be the chiefest, shall be servant of all.

For even the Son of man came not to be ministered unto, but to minister, and to give his life a ransom for many.

Mark 10:35-45

I must work the works of him that sent me, while it is day: the night cometh, when no man can work.

John 9:4

And it came to pass, that after three days they found him in the temple, sitting in the midst of the doctors, both hearing them, and asking them questions.

And all that heard him were astonished at his understanding and answers.

And when they saw him, they were amazed: and his mother said unto him, Son, why hast thou thus dealt with us? behold, thy father and I have sought thee sorrowing.

And he said unto them, How is it that ye sought me? wist ye not that I must be about my Father's business?

Luke 2:46-49

This man was instructed in the way of the Lord; and being fervent in the spirit, he spake and taught diligently the things of the Lord, knowing only the baptism of John.

Acts 18:25

Know ye not that they which run in a race run all, but one receiveth the prize? So run, that ye may obtain.

I Corinthians 9:24

Again, the devil taketh him up into an exceeding high mountain, and sheweth him all the kingdoms of the world, and the glory of them;

And saith unto him, All these things will I give thee, if thou wilt fall down and worship me.

Then saith Jesus unto him, Get thee hence, Satan: for it is written, Thou shalt worship the Lord thy God, and him only shalt thou serve.

Matthew 4:8-10

But covet earnestly the best gifts: and yet shew I unto you a more excellent way.

I Corinthians 12:31

How can ye believe, which receive honour one of another, and seek not the honour that (cometh) from God only?

John 5:44

All therefore whatsoever they bid you observe, that observe and do; but do not ye after their works: for they say, and do not.

But all their works they do for to be seen of men: they make broad their phylacteries, and enlarge the borders of their garments,

But be not ye called Rabbi: for one is your Master, even Christ; and all ye are brethren.

Matthew 23:3, 5, 8

But he that is greatest among you shall be your servant.

And whosoever shall exalt himself shall be abased; and he that shall humble himself shall be exalted.

Matthew 23:11, 12

Be thou diligent to know the state of thy flocks, (and) look well to thy herds.

Proverbs 27:23

Thou shalt not covet thy neighbour's house, thou shalt not covet thy neighbor's wife, nor his manservant, nor his maidservant, nor his ox, nor his ass, nor any thing that (is) thy neighbor's

Exodus 20:17

And he came to Capernaum: and being in the house he asked them, What was it that ye disputed among yourselves by the way?

But they held their peace: for by the way they had disputed among themselves, who (should be) the greatest.

And he sat down, and called the twelve, and saith unto them, If any man desire to be first, (the same) shall be last of all, and servant of all.

And he took a child, and set him in the midst of them: and when he had taken him in his arms, he said unto them,

Whosoever shall receive one of such children in my name, receiveth me: and whosoever shall receive me, receiveth not me, but him that sent me.

Mark 9:33-37

Even so ye, forasmuch as ye are zealous of spiritual (gifts), seek that ye may excel to the edifying of the church.

I Corinthians 14:12

For Zion's sake will I not hold my peace, and for Jerusalem's sake I will not rest, until the righteousness thereof go forth as brightness, and the salvation thereof as a lamp (that) burneth.

Isaiah 62:1

Their inward thought (is, that) their houses (shall continue) for ever, (and) their dwelling places to all generations; they call (their) lands after their own names.

Nevertheless man (being) in honour abideth not: he is like the beasts (that) perish.

This their way (is) their folly: yet their posterity approve their sayings. Selah.

Psalms 49:11-13

Diligence & Perseverance

Seek the LORD and his strength, seek his face continually.

I Chronicles 16:11

But he that shall endure unto the end, the same shall be saved.

Matthew 24:13

Stand fast therefore in the liberty wherewith Christ hath made us free, and be not entangled again with the yoke of bondage.

Galatians 5:1

And let us not be weary in well doing: for in due season we shall reap, if we faint not.

Galatians 6:9

He that descended is the same also that ascended up far above all heavens, that he might fill all things.

Till we all come in the unity of the faith, and of the knowledge of the Son of God, unto a perfect man, unto the measure of the stature of the fulness of Christ:

That we (henceforth) be no more children, tossed to and fro, and carried about with every wind of doctrine, by the sleight of men, (and) cunning craftiness, whereby they lie in wait to deceive;

But speaking the truth in love, may grow up into him in all things, which is the head, even Christ:
Ephesians 4:10, 13-15

But ye, brethren, be not weary in well doing.
II Thessalonians 3:13

Thou therefore, my son, be strong in the grace that is in Christ Jesus.
II Timothy 2:1

But continue thou in the things which thou hast learned and hast been assured of, knowing of whom thou hast learned (them);
II Timothy 3:14

But Christ as a son over his own house; whose house are we, if we hold fast the confidence and the rejoicing of the hope firm unto the end.
Wherefore (as the Holy Ghost saith, To day if ye will hear his voice,
Harden not your hearts, as in the provocation, in the day of temptation in the wilderness:
Hebrews 3:6-8

Wherefore seeing we also are compassed about with so great a cloud of witnesses, let us lay aside every weight, and the sin which doth so easily beset (us), and let us run with patience the race that is set before us,
Hebrews 12:1

Wherefore gird up the loins of your mind, be sober, and hope to the end for the grace that is to be brought unto you at the revelation of Jesus Christ;

I Peter 1:13

Be sober, be vigilant; because your adversary the devil, as a roaring lion, walketh about, seeking whom he may devour:

I Peter 5:8

Wherefore the rather, brethren, give diligence to make your calling and election sure: for if ye do these things, ye shall never fall:

For so an entrance shall be ministered unto you abundantly into the everlasting kingdom of our Lord and Saviour Jesus Christ.

II Peter 1:10, 11

Seest thou a man diligent in his business? he shall stand before kings; he shall not stand before mean (men).

Proverbs 22:29

Therefore turn thou to thy God: keep mercy and judgment, and wait on thy God continually.

Hosea 12:6

And the Lord said, Simon, Simon, behold, Satan hath desired (to have) you, that he may sift (you) as wheat:

But I have prayed for thee, that thy faith fail not: and when thou are converted, strenghten thy brethren.

Luke 22:31, 32

Then said Jesus to those Jews which believed on him, If ye continue in my word, (then) are ye my disciples indeed;

And ye shall know the truth, and the truth shall make you free.

John 8:31, 32

And I give unto them eternal life; and they shall never perish, neither shall any (man) pluck them out of my hand.

My Father, which gave (them) me, is greater than all; and no (man) is able to pluck (them) out of my Father's hand.

John 10:28, 29

Abide in me, and I in you. As the branch cannot bear fruit of itself, except it abide in the vine; no more can ye, except ye abide in me.

I am the vine, ye (are) the branches: He that abideth in me, and I in him, the same bringeth forth much fruit: for without me ye can do nothing.

If ye abide in me, and my words abide in you, ye shall ask what ye will, and it shall be done unto you.

Herein is my Father glorified, that ye bear much fruit; so shall ye be my disciples.

As the Father hath loved me, so have I loved you: continue ye in my love.

John 15:4, 5, 7-9

Who shall separate us from the love of Christ? (shall) tribulation, or distress, or persecution, or famine, or nakedness, or peril, or sword?

As it is written, For thy sake we are killed all the day long; we are accounted as sheep for the slaughter.

Nay, in all these things we are more than conquerors through him that loved us.

For I am persuaded, that neither death, nor life, nor angels, nor principalities, nor powers, nor things present, nor things to come,

Nor height, nor depth, nor any other creature, shall be able to separate us from the love of God, which is in Christ Jesus our Lord.

Romans 8:35-39

Moreover, brethren, I declare unto you the gospel which I preached unto you, which also ye have received, and wherein ye stand;

By which also ye are saved, if ye keep in memory what I preached unto you, unless ye have believed in vain.

I Corinthians 15:1, 2

Therefore, my beloved brethren, be ye stedfast, unmoveable, always abounding in the work of the Lord, forasmuch as ye know that your labour is not in vain in the Lord.

I Corinthians 15:58

Only let your conversation be as it becometh the gospel of Christ: that whether I come and see you, or else be absent, I may hear of your affairs, that ye stand fast in one spirit, with one mind striving together for the faith of the gospel;

Philippians 1:27

Prove all things; hold fast that which is good.

I Thessalonians 5:21

Ye therefore, beloved, seeing ye know (these things) before, beware lest ye also, being led away with the error of the wicked, fall from your own stedfastness.

But grow in grace, and (in) the knowledge of our Lord and Saviour Jesus Christ. To him (be) glory both now and for ever. Amen.

II Peter 3:17, 18

And when they had preached the gospel to that city, and had taught many, they returned again to Lystra, and (to) Iconium, and Antioch,

Confirming the souls of the disciples, (and) exhorting them to continue in the faith, and that we must through much tribulation enter into the kingdom of God.

Acts 14:21, 22

The thoughts of the diligent (tend) only to plenteousness; but of every one (that is) hasty only to want.

Proverbs 21:5

The soul of the sluggard desireth, and (hath) nothing: but the soul of the diligent shall be made fat.

Proverbs 13:4

He becometh poor that dealeth (with) a slack hand: but the hand of the diligent maketh rich.

Proverbs 10:4

Integrity

The just (man) walketh in his integrity: his children (are) blessed after him.

Proverbs 20:7

To do justice and judgment (is) more acceptable to the LORD than sacrifice.

Proverbs 21:3

[(A Psalm) of David.] Judge me, O LORD; for I have walked in mine integrity: I have trusted also in the LORD; (therefore) I shall not slide.

Examine me, O LORD and prove me; try my reins and my heart.

For thy lovingkindness (is) before mine eyes: and I have walked in thy truth.

Psalms 26:1-3

The integrity of the upright shall guide them: but the perverseness of transgressors shall destroy them.

Riches profit not in the day of wrath: but righteousness delivereth from death.

The righteousness of the perfect shall direct his way: but the wicked shall fall by his own wickedness.

Proverbs 11:3-5

Judge not, that ye be not judged.

For with what judgment ye judge, ye shall be judged: and with what measure ye mete, it shall be measured to you again.

And why beholdest thou the mote that is in thy brother's eye, but considerest not the beam that is in thine own eye?

Or how wilt thou say to thy brother, Let me pull out the mote out of thine eye; and, behold, a beam (is) in thine own eye?

Thou hypocrite, first cast out the beam out of thine own eye; and then shalt thou see clearly to cast out the mote out of thy brother's eye.

Matthew 7:1-5

But the path of the just (is) as the shining light, that shineth more and more unto the perfect day.

Proverbs 4:18

My lips shall not speak wickedness, nor my tongue utter deceit.

God forbid that I should justify you: till I die I will not remove mine integrity from me.

My righteousness I hold fast, and will not let it go: my heart shall not reproach (me) so long as I live.

Job 27:4-6

But if a man be just, and do that which is lawful and right,

(And) hath not eaten upon the mountains, neither hath lifted up his eyes to the idols of the house of Israel, neither hath defiled his neighbour's wife, neither hath come near to a menstruous woman,

And hath not oppressed any, (but) hath restored to the debtor his pledge, hath spoiled none by violence, hath given his bread to the hungry, and hath covered the naked with a garment;

He (that) hath not given forth upon usury, neither hath taken any increase, (that) hath withdrawn his hand from iniquity, hath executed true judgement between man and man,

Hath walked in my statutes, and hath kept my judgments, to deal truly; he (is) just, he shall surely live, saith the Lord GOD.

Ezekiel 18:5-9

He that walketh righteously, and speaketh uprightly; he that despiseth the gain of oppressions, that shaketh his hands from holding of bribes, that stoppeth his ears from hearing of blood, and shutteth his eyes from seeing evil;

He shall dwell on high: his place of defence (shall be) the munitions of rocks: bread shall be given him; his waters (shall be) sure.

Isaiah 33:15, 16

Hearken to me, ye that follow after righteousness, ye that seek the LORD: look unto the rock (whence) ye are hewn, and to the hole of the pit (whence) ye are digged.

Isaiah 51:1

For if ye throughly amend your ways and your doings; if ye throughly execute judgment between a man and his neighbour;

If ye oppress not the stranger, the fatherless, and the widow, and shed not innocent blood in this place, neither walk after other gods to your hurt:

Then will I cause you to dwell in this place, in the land that I gave to your fathers, for ever and ever.

Jeremiah 7:5-7

O LORD my God, if I have done this; if there be iniquity in my hands;

If I have rewarded evil unto him that was at peace with me; (yea, I have delivered him that without cause is mine enemy:)

Let the enemy persecute my soul, and take (it); yea, let him tread down my life upon the earth, and lay mine honour in the dust. Selah.

Arise, O LORD, in thine anger, lift up thyself because of the rage of mine enemies: and awake for me (to) the judgment (that) thou hast commanded.

The LORD shall judge the people: judge me, O LORD, according to my righteousness, and according to mine integrity (that is) in me.

Psalms 7:3-6, 8

And he said unto them, Exact no more than that which is appointed you.

And the soldiers likewise demanded of him, saying, And what shall we do? And he said unto them, Do violence to no man, neither accuse (any) falsely; and be content with your wages.

Luke 3:13, 14

(A Psalm of David.) LORD, who shall abide in thy tabernacle? who shall dwell in thy holy hill?

He that walketh uprightly, and worketh righteousness, and speaketh the truth in his heart.

(He that) backbiteth not with his tongue, nor doeth evil to his neighbour, nor taketh up a reproach against his neighbour.

In whose eyes a vile person is contemned; but he honoureth them that fear the LORD. (He that) sweareth to (his own) hurt, and changeth not.

(He that) putteth not out his money to usury, nor taketh reward against the innocent. He that doeth these (things) shall never be moved.

Psalms 15:1-5

He that is faithful in that which is least is faithful also in much: and he that is unjust in the least is unjust also in much.

Luke 16:10

But woe unto you, Pharisees! for ye tithe mint and rue and all manner of herbs, and pass over judgment and the love of God: these ought ye to have done, and not to leave the other undone.

Luke 11:42

My son, if thou wilt receive my words, and hide my commandments with thee;

So that thou incline thine ear unto wisdom, (and) apply thine heart to understanding;

Yea, if thou criest after knowledge, (and) liftest up thy voice for understanding;

Then shalt thou understand the fear of the LORD, and find the knowledge of God.

He layeth up sound wisdom for the righteous: (he is) a buckler to them that walk uprightly.

Then shalt thou understand righteousness, and judgment, and equity; (yea), every good path.

Proverbs 2:1-3, 5, 7, 9

Let not mercy and truth forsake thee: bind them about thy neck; write them upon the table of thine heart:

So shalt thou find favour and good understanding in the sight of God and man.

Proverbs 3:3, 4

Though he slay me, yet will I trust in him: but I will maintain mine own ways before him.

Behold now, I have ordered (my) cause; I know that I shall be justified.

Job 13:15, 18

Let thine eyes look right on, and let thine eyelids look straight before thee.

Ponder the path of thy feet, and let all thy ways be established.

Turn not to the right hand nor to the left: remove thy foot from evil.

Proverbs 4:25-27

Lying lips (are) abomination to the LORD: but they that deal truly (are) his delight.

Proverbs 12:22

The discretion of a man deferreth his anger; and (it is) his glory to pass over a transgression.

Proverbs 19:11

And Zacchaeus stood, and said unto the Lord; Behold, Lord, the half of my goods I give to the poor; and if I taken any thing from any man by false accusation, I restore (him) fourfold.

And Jesus said unto him, This day is salvation come to this house, forsomuch as he also is a son of Abraham.

For the Son of man is come to seek and to save that which was lost.

Luke 19:8-10

Biblical Foundations For Your Business Success...

Personal Relationship With Jesus Christ

For God so loved the world, that he gave his only begotten Son, that whosoever believeth in him should not perish, but have everlasting life.

For God sent not his Son into the world to condemn the world; but that the world through him might be saved.

He that believeth on him is not condemned: but he that believeth not is condemned already, because he hath not believed in the name of the only begotten Son of God.

John 3:16-18

There was a man of the Pharisees, named Nicodemus, a ruler of the Jews:

The same came to Jesus by night, and said unto him, Rabbi, we know that thou art a teacher come from God: for no man can do these miracles that thou doest, except God be with him.

Jesus answered and said unto him, Verily, verily, I say unto thee, Except a man be born again, he cannot see the kingdom of God.

Nicodemus saith unto him, How can a man be born when he is old? can he enter the second time into his mother's womb, and be born?

Jesus answered, Verily, verily, I say unto thee, Except a man be born of water and (of) the Spirit, he cannot enter into the kingdom of God.

That which is born of the flesh is flesh; and that which is born of the Spirit is spirit.

Marvel not that I said unto thee, Ye must be born again.

The wind bloweth where it listeth, and thou hearest the sound thereof, but canst not tell whence it cometh, and whither it goeth: so is every one that is born of the Spirit.

John 3:1-8

He that believeth on the Son hath everlasting life: and he that believeth not the Son shall not see life; but the wrath of God abideth on him.

John 3:36

The thief cometh not, but for to steal, and to kill, and to destroy: I am come that they might have life, and that they might have (it) more abundantly.

John 10:10

But as many as received him, to them gave he power to become the sons of God, (even) to them that believe on his name:

John 1:12

For all have sinned, and come short of the glory of God;

Romans 3:23

For the wages of sin (is) death; but the gift of God (is) eternal life through Jesus Christ our Lord.

Romans 6:23

But God commendeth his love toward us, in that, while we were yet sinners, Christ died for us.

Romans 5:8

Jesus saith unto him, I am the way, the truth, and the life: no man cometh unto the Father, but by me.

John 14:6

For by grace are ye saved through faith; and that not of yourselves: (it is) the gift of God:

Not of works, lest any man should boast.

Ephesians 2:8, 9

That if thou shalt confess with thy mouth the Lord Jesus, and shalt believe in thine heart that God hath raised him from the dead, thou shalt be saved.

For with the heart man believeth unto righteousness; and with the mouth confession is made unto salvation.

For the scripture saith, Whosoever believeth on him shall not be ashamed.

For there is no difference between the Jew and the Greek: for the same Lord over all is rich unto all that call upon him.

For whosoever shall call upon the name of the Lord shall be saved.

Romans 10:9-13

Behold, I stand at the door, and knock: if any man hear my voice, and open the door, I will come in to him, and will sup with him, and he with me.

Revelation 3:20

For the Son of man is come to seek and to save that which was lost.

Luke 19:10

Neither is there salvation in any other: for there is none other name under heaven given among men, whereby we must be saved.

Acts 4:12

If we say that we have no sin, we deceive ourselves, and the truth is not in us.

If we confess our sins, he is faithful and just to forgive us (our) sins, and to cleanse us from all unrighteousness.

If we say that we have not sinned, we make him a liar, and his word is not in us.

I John 1:8-10

Therefore if any man (be) in Christ (he is) a new creature: old things are passed away; behold, all things are become new.

II Corinthians 5:17

Verily, verily, I say unto you, He that heareth my word, and believeth on him that sent me, hath everlasting life, and shall not come into condemnation; but is passed from death unto life.

John 5:24

Jesus said unto her, I am the resurrection, and the life: he that believeth in me, though he were dead, yet shall he live:

John 11:25

But these are written, that ye might believe that Jesus is the Christ, the Son of God; and that believing ye might have life through his name.

John 20:31

Then Peter said unto them, Repent, and be baptized every one of you in the name of Jesus Christ for the remission of sins, and ye shall receive the gift of the Holy Ghost.

Acts 2:38

For I am not ashamed of the gospel of Christ: for it is the power of God unto salvation to every one that believeth; to the Jew first, and also to the Greek.

Romans 1:16

Prayer & Devotional Life

And when thou prayest, thou shalt not be as the hypocrites (are): for they love to pray standing in the synagogues and in the corners of the streets, that they may be seen of men. Verily I say unto you, They have their reward.

But thou, when thou prayest, enter into thy closet, and when thou hast shut thy door, pray to thy Father which is in secret; and thy Father which seeth in secret shall reward thee openly.

But when ye pray, use not vain repetitions, as the heathen (do): for they think that they shall be heard for their much speaking.

Be not ye therefore like unto them: for your Father knoweth what things ye have need of, before ye ask him.

Matthew 6:5-8

After this manner therefore pray ye: Our Father which art in heaven, Hallowed be thy name.

Thy kingdom come. Thy will be done in earth, as (it is) in heaven.

Give us this day our daily bread.

And forgive us our debts, as we forgive our debtors.

And lead us not into temptation, but deliver us from evil: For thine is the kingdom, and the power, and the glory, for ever. Amen.

Matthew 6:9-13

And he spake a parable unto them (to this end), that men ought always to pray, and not to faint;
Luke 18:1

Is any among you afflicted? let him pray. Is any merry? let him sing psalms.

Is any sick among you? let him call for the elders of the church; and let them pray over him, anointing him with oil in the name of the Lord:

And the prayer of faith shall save the sick, and the Lord shall raise him up; and if he have committed sins, they shall be forgiven him.

Confess (your) faults one to another, and pray one for another, that ye may be healed. The effectual fervent prayer of a righteous man availeth much.
James 5:13-16

Likewise the Spirit also helpeth our infirmities: for we know not what we should pray for as we ought: but the Spirit itself maketh intercession for us with groanings which cannot be uttered.

And he that searcheth the hearts knoweth what (is) the mind of the Spirit, because he maketh intercession for the saints according to (the will of) God.

Romans 8:26, 27

Seek the LORD and his strength, seek his face continually.

I Chronicles 16:11

And this is the confidence that we have in him, that, if we ask any thing according to his will, he heareth us:

And if we know that he hear us, whatsoever we ask, we know that we have the petitions that we desired of him.

I John 5:14, 15

And he spake a parable unto them (to this end), that men ought always to pray, and not to faint;

Luke 18:1

Watch ye therefore, and pray always, that ye may be accounted worthy to escape all these things that shall come to pass, and to stand before the Son of man.

Luke 21:36

Thy word have I hid in mine heart, that I might not sin against thee.

Psalms 119:11

Let the words of my mouth, and the meditation of my heart, be acceptable in thy sight, O LORD, my strength, and my redeemer.

Psalms 19:14

(NUN.) Thy word (is) a lamp unto my feet, and a light unto my path.

Psalms 119:105

If my people, which are called by my name, shall humble themselves, and pray, and seek my face, and turn from their wicked ways; then will I hear from heaven, and will forgive their sin, and will heal their land.

II Chronicles 7:14

But if from thence thou shalt seek the LORD thy God, thou shalt find (him), if thou seek him with all thy heart and with all thy soul.

When thou art in tribulation, and all these things are come upon thee, (even) in the latter days, if thou turn to the LORD thy God, and shalt be obedient unto his voice;

[For the LORD thy God (is) a merciful God;] he will not forsake thee, neither destroy thee, nor forget the covenant of thy fathers which he sware unto them.

Deuteronomy 4:29-31

Thou shalt make thy prayer unto him, and he shall hear thee, and thou shalt pay thy vows.

Job 22:27

As for me, I will call upon God; and the LORD shall save me.

Evening, and morning, and at noon, will I pray, and cry aloud: and he shall hear my voice.

Psalms 55:16, 17

For thou, Lord (art) good, and ready to forgive; and plenteous in mercy unto all them that call upon thee.

Give ear, O LORD, unto my prayer; and attend to the voice of my supplications.

In the day of my trouble I will call upon thee: for thou wilt answer me.

Psalms 86:5-7

The fear of the LORD (is) the instruction of wisdom; and before honour (is) humility.

Proverbs 15:33

The sacrifice of the wicked (is) an abomination to the LORD: but the prayer of the upright (is) his delight.

Proverbs 15:8

Seek ye the LORD while he may be found, call ye upon him while he is near:

Isaiah 55:6

Then shall ye call upon me, and ye shall go and pray unto me, and I will hearken unto you.

And ye shall seek me, and find (me), when ye shall search for me with all your heart.

Jeremiah 29:12, 13

Call unto me, and I will answer thee, and shew thee great and mighty things, which thou knowest not.

Jeremiah 33:3

Again I say unto you, That if two of you shall agree on earth as touching any thing that they shall ask, it shall be done for them of my Father which is in heaven.

For where two or three are gathered together in my name, there am I in the midst of them.

Matthew 18:19, 20

Therefore I say unto you, What things soever ye desire, when ye pray, believe that ye receive (them), and ye shall have (them).

And when ye stand praying, forgive, if ye have ought against any: that your Father also which is in heaven may forgive you your trespasses.

Mark 11:24, 25

And in that day ye shall ask me nothing. Verily, verily, I say unto you, Whatsoever ye shall ask the Father in my name, he will give (it) you.

Hitherto have ye asked nothing in my name: ask, and ye shall receive, that your joy may be full.

At that day ye shall ask in my name: and I say not unto you, that I will pray the Father for you:

John 16:23, 24, 26

Let us therefore come boldly unto the throne of grace, that we may obtain mercy, and find grace to help in time of need.

Hebrews 4:16

And whatsoever we ask, we receive of him, because we keep his commandments, and do those things that are pleasing in his sight.

I John 3:22

Balanced Family Life

And the LORD God said, (It is) not good that the man should be alone; I will make him an help meet for him.

And Adam said, This (is) now bone of my bones, and flesh of my flesh: she shall be called Woman, because she was taken out of Man.

Therefore shall a man leave his father and his mother, and shall cleave unto his wife: and they shall be one flesh.

Genesis 2:18, 23, 24

Who can find a virtuous woman? for her price (is) far above rubies.

The heart of her husband doth safely trust in her, so that he shall have no need of spoil.

She will do him good and not evil all the days of her life.

Proverbs 31:10-12

Wives, submit yourselves unto your own husbands, as unto the Lord.

For the husband is the head of the wife, even as Christ is the head of the church: and he is the saviour of the body.

Therefore as the church is subject unto Christ, so (let) the wives (be) to their own husbands in every thing.

Husbands, love your wives, even as Christ also loved the church, and gave himself for it;

So ought men to love their wives as their own bodies. He that loveth his wife loveth himself.

Ephesians 5:22-25, 28

And Ruth said, Entreat me not to leave thee, (or) to return from following after thee: for whither thou goest, I will go; and where thou lodgest, I will lodge: thy people (shall be) my people, and thy God my God:

Where thou diest, will I die, and there will I be buried: the LORD do so to me, and more also, (if ought) but death part thee and me.

Ruth 1:16, 17

Likewise, ye wives, (be) in subjection to your own husbands; that, if any obey not the word, they also may without the word be won by the conversation of the wives;

While they behold your chaste conversation (coupled) with fear.

I Peter 3:1, 2

Likewise, ye husbands, dwell with (them) according to knowledge, giving honour unto the wife, as unto the weaker vessel, and as being heirs together of the grace of life; that your prayers be not hindered.

I Peter 3:7

The Pharisees also came unto him, tempting him, and saying unto him, Is it lawful for a man to put away his wife for every cause?

And he answered and said unto them, Have ye not read, that he which made (them) at the beginning made them male and female,

And said, For this cause shall a man leave father and mother, and shall cleave to his wife: and they twain shall be one flesh?

Wherefore they are no more twain, but one flesh. What therefore God hath joined together, let not man put asunder.

Matthew 19:3-6

It hath been said, Whosoever shall put away his wife, let him give her a writing of divorcement:

But I say unto you, That whosoever shall put away his wife, saving for the cause of fornication, causeth her to commit adultery: and whosoever shall marry her that is divorced committeth adultery.

Matthew 5:31, 32

Children, obey your parents in the Lord: for this is right.

Honour thy father and mother; which is the first commandment with promise;

That it may be well with thee, and thou mayest live long on the earth.

And, ye fathers, provoke not your children to wrath: but bring them up in the nurture and admonition of the Lord.

Ephesians 6:1-4

A wise son maketh a glad father: but a foolish man despiseth his mother.

Proverbs 15:20

He that spareth his rod hateth his son: but he that loveth him chasteneth him betimes.

Proverbs 13:24

Honour thy father and thy mother: that thy days may be long upon the land which the LORD thy God giveth thee.

Exodus 20:12

Peace Of Mind

Blessed (are) the peacemakers: for they shall be called the children of God.

Matthew 5:9

These things I have spoken unto you, that in me ye might have peace. In the world ye shall have tribulation: but be of good cheer; I have overcome the world.

John 16:33

Peace I leave with you, my peace I give unto you: not as the world giveth, give I unto you. Let not your heart be troubled neither let it be afraid.

John 14:27

Therefore being justified by faith, we have peace with God through our Lord Jesus Christ:

Romans 5:1

Therefore take no thought, saying, What shall we eat? or, What shall we drink? or, Wherewithal shall we be clothed?

(For after all these things do the Gentiles seek:) for your heavenly Father knoweth that ye have need of all these things.

But seek ye first the kingdom of God, and his righteousness; and all these things shall be added unto you.

Take therefore no thought for the morrow: for the morrow shall take thought for the things of itself. Sufficient unto the day (is) the evil thereof.

Matthew 6:31-34

He that dwelleth in the secret place of the most High shall abide under the shadow of the Almighty.

I will say of the LORD, (He is) my refuge and my fortress: my God; in him will I trust.

Psalms 91:1, 2

Create in me a clean heart, O God; and renew a right spirit within me.

Cast me not away from thy presence; and take not thy holy spirit from me.

Restore unto me the joy of thy salvation; and uphold me (with thy) free spirit.

(Then) will I teach transgressors thy ways; and sinners shall be converted unto thee.

Psalms 51:10-13

Better (is) little with the fear of the LORD than great treasure and trouble therewith.

Proverbs 15:16

Salt (is) good: but if the salt have lost his saltness, wherewith will ye season it? Have salt in yourselves, and have peace one with another.

Mark 9:50

Finally, brethren, farewell. Be perfect, be of good comfort, be of one mind, live in peace; and the God of love and peace shall be with you.

Greet one another with an holy kiss.

II Corinthians 13:11, 12

Be careful for nothing; but in every thing by prayer and supplication with thanksgiving let your requests be made known unto God.

And the peace of God, which passeth all understanding, shall keep your hearts and minds through Christ Jesus.

Finally, brethren, whatsoever things are true, whatsoever things (are) honest, whatsoever things (are) just, whatsoever things (are) pure, whatsoever things (are) lovely, whatsoever things (are) of good report; if (there be) any virtue, and if (there be) any praise, think on these things.

Those things, which ye have both learned, and received, and heard, and seen in me, do: and the God of peace shall be with you.

Phillippians 4:6-9

And let the peace of God rule in your hearts, to the which also ye are called in one body; and be ye thankful.

Colossians 3:15

Wherefore comfort yourselves together, and edify one another, even as also ye do.

And we beseech you, brethren, to know them which labour among you, and are over you in the Lord, and admonish you;

And to esteem them very highly in love for their work's sake. (And) be at peace among yourselves.

I Thessalonians 5:11-13

But the wisdom that is from above is first pure, then peaceable, gentle, (and) easy to be intreated, full of mercy and good fruits, without partiality, and without hypocrisy.

And the fruit of righteousness is sown in peace of them that make peace.

James 3:17, 18

Follow peace with all (men), and holiness, without which no man shall see the Lord:

Hebrews 12:14

Flee also youthful lusts: but follow righteousness, faith, charity, peace, with them that call on the Lord out of a pure heart.

II Timothy 2:22

Now the Lord of peace himself give you peace always by all means. The Lord (be) with you all.

II Thessalonians 3:16

For he that will love life, and see good days, let him refrain his tongue from evil, and his lips that they speak no guile:

Let him eschew evil, and do good; let him seek peace, and ensue it.

I Peter 3:10, 11

Thou wilt keep (him) in perfect peace, (whose) mind (is) stayed (on thee): because he trusteth in thee.

Isaiah 26:3

Jesus saith unto him, I am the way, the truth, and the life: no man cometh unto the Father, but by me.

John 14:6

The LORD will give strength unto his people; the LORD will bless his people with peace.

Psalms 29:11

When a man's ways please the LORD, he maketh even his enemies to be at peace with him.

Proverbs 16:7

In the beginning God created the heaven and the earth.

And the earth was without form, and void; and darkness was upon the face of the deep. And the spirit of God moved upon the face of the waters.

And God said, Let there be light: and there was light.

Genesis 1:1-3

Better (is) an handful (with) quietness, than both the hands full (with) travail and vexation of spirit.

Ecclesiastes 4:6

If it be possible, as much as lieth in you, live peaceably with all men.

Romans 12:18

Let us therefore follow after the things which make for peace, and things wherewith one may edify another.

Romans 14:19

For God is not (the author) of confusion, but of peace, as in all churches of the saints.

I Corinthians 14:33

(It is of) the LORD'S mercies that we are not consumed, because his compassions fail not.

(They are) new every morning: great (is) thy faithfulness.

The LORD (is) my portion, saith my soul; therefore will I hope in him.

Lamentations 3:22-24

(I had fainted), unless I had believed to see the goodness of the LORD in the land of the living.

Wait on the LORD: be of good courage, and he shall strengthen thine heart: wait, I say, on the LORD.

Psalms 27:13, 14

Thou (art) my hiding place and my shield:
I hope in thy word.

Psalms 119:114

Moral Uprightness

But seek ye first the kingdom of God, and
his righteousness; and all these things shall be added unto you.

Matthew 6:33

Love not the world, neither the things (that
are) in the world. If any man love the world, the
love of the Father is not in him.

For all that (is) in the world, the lust of the
flesh, and the lust of the eyes, and the pride of
life, is not of the Father, but is of the world.

And the world passeth away, and the lust
thereof: but he that doeth the will of God abideth
for ever.

I John 2:15-17

My little children, these things write I unto
you, that ye sin not. And if any man sin, we have an
advocate with the Father, Jesus Christ the righteous:

And he is the propitiation for our sins: and
not for ours only, but also for (the sins of) the
whole world.

And hereby we do know that we know him,
if we keep his commandments.

He that saith, I know him, and keepeth not
his commandments, is a liar, and the truth is not
in him.

But whoso keepeth his word, in him verily
is the love of God perfected: hereby know we that
we are in him.

He that saith he abideth in him ought himself also so to walk, even as he walked.

I John 2:1-6

Who shall ascend into the hill of the LORD? or who shall stand in his holy place?

He that hath clean hands, and a pure heart; who hath not lifted up his soul unto vanity, nor sworn deceitfully.

He shall receive the blessing from the LORD, and righteousness from the God of his salvation.

Psalms 24:3-5

Blessed (is) the man that walketh not in the counsel of the ungodly, nor standeth in the way of sinners, nor sitteth in the seat of the scornful.

But his delight (is) in the law of the LORD; and in his law doth he meditate day and night.

And he shall be like a tree planted by the rivers of water, that bringeth forth his fruit in his season; his leaf also shall not wither; and whatsoever he doeth shall prosper.

Psalms 1:1-3

My son, keep my words, and lay up my commandments with thee.

Keep my commandments, and live; and my law as the apple of thine eye.

Bind them upon thy fingers, write them upon the table of thine heart.

Proverbs 7:1-3

He that walketh righteously, and speaketh
uprightly; he that despiseth the gain of oppressions,
that shaketh his hands from holding of bribes, that
stoppeth his ears from hearing of blood, and shutteth his eyes from seeing evil;

He shall dwell on high: his place of defence
(shall be) the munitions of rocks: bread shall be
given him; his waters (shall be) sure.

Isaiah 33:15, 16

Righteousness exalteth a nation: but sin (is)
a reproach to any people.

Proverbs 14:34

Wisdom strengtheneth the wise more than ten
mighty men which are in the city.

For (there is) not a just man upon earth, that
doeth good, and sinneth not.

Ecclesiastes 7:19, 20

If ye love me, keep my commandments.

John 14:15

And why call ye me, Lord, Lord, and do not
the things which I say?

Whosoever cometh to me, and heareth my
sayings, and doeth them, I will shew you to whom
he is like:

He is like a man which built an house, and
digged deep, and laid the foundation on a rock: and
when the flood arose, the stream beat vehemently
upon that house, and could not shake it: for it was
founded upon a rock.

Luke 6:46-48

Teach me to do thy will; for thou (art) my God: thy spirit (is) good; lead me into the land of uprightness.

Psalms 143:10

And if thou wilt walk in my ways, to keep my statutes and my commandments, as thy father David did walk, then I will lengthen thy days.

I Kings 3:14

Blessed (is) the man that walketh not in the counsel of the ungodly, nor standeth in the way of sinners, nor sitteth in the seat of the scornful.
But his delight (is) in the law of the LORD; and in his law doth he meditate day and night.
And he shall be like a tree planted by the rivers of water, that bringeth forth his fruit in his season; his leaf also shall not wither; and whatsoever he doeth shall prosper.

Psalms 1:1-3

The fear of the LORD (is) the beginning of wisdom: a good understanding have all they that do (his commandments): his praise endureth for ever.

Psalms 111:10

Praise ye the LORD. Blessed (is) the man (that) feareth the LORD, (that) delighteth greatly in his commandments.

Psalms 112:1

**In righteousness shalt thou be established:
thou shalt be far from oppression; for thou shalt not
fear: and from terror; for it shall not come near thee.**

Isaiah 54:14

Emotional Stability

For God hath not given us the spirit of fear;
but of power, and of love, and of a sound mind.

II Timothy 1:7

For ye have not received the spirit of bondage
again to fear; but ye have received the Spirit of
adoption, whereby we cry, Abba, Father.

Romans 8:15

Therefore I say unto you, Take no thought for
your life, what ye shall eat, or what ye shall drink;
nor yet for your body, what ye shall put on. Is not the
life more than meat, and the body than raiment?

Behold the fowls of the air: for they sow not,
neither do they reap, nor gather into barns; yet your
heavenly Father feedeth them. Are ye not much
better than they?

Which of you by taking thought can add one
cubit unto his stature?

And why take ye thought for raiment? Consider the lilies of the field, how they grow; they toil
not, neither do they spin:

And yet I say unto you, That even Solomon
in all his glory was not arrayed like one of these.

Wherefore, if God so clothe the grass of the
field, which to day is, and to morrow is cast into the
oven, (shall he) not much more (clothe) you, O ye
of little faith?

Therefore take no thought, saying, What
shall we eat? or, What shall we drink? or,
Wherewithal shall we be clothed?

(For after all these things do the Gentiles seek:) for your heavenly Father knoweth that ye have need of all these things.

But seek ye first the kingdom of God, and his righteousness; and all these things shall be added unto you.

Take therefore no thought for the morrow: for the morrow shall take thought for the things of itself. Sufficient unto the day (is) the evil thereof.

Matthew 6:25-34

Be ye angry, and sin not: let not the sun go down upon your wrath:

Neither give place to the devil.

Ephesians 4:26, 27

Let all bitterness, and wrath, and anger, and clamour, and evil speaking, be put away from you, with all malice:

And be ye kind one to another, tenderhearted, forgiving one another, even as God for Christ's sake hath forgiven you.

Ephesians 4:31, 32

But the fruit of the Spirit is love, joy, peace, longsuffering, gentleness, goodness, faith,

Meekness, temperance: against such there is no law.

Galatians 5:22, 23

Rejoice in the Lord alway: (and) again I say, Rejoice.

Be careful for nothing; but in every thing by prayer and supplication with thanksgiving let your requests be made known unto God.

And the peace of God, which passeth all understanding, shall keep your hearts and minds through Christ Jesus.

Finally, brethren, whatsoever things are true, whatsoever things (are) honest, whatsoever things (are) just, whatsoever things (are) pure, whatsoever things (are) lovely, whatsoever things (are) of good report; if (there be) any virtue, and if (there be) any praise, think on these things.

Those things, which ye have both learned, and received, and heard, and seen in me, do: and the God of peace shall be with you.

Philippians 4:4, 6-9

[(A Psalm) of David.] Fret not thyself because of evildoers, neither be thou envious against the workers of iniquity.

For they shall soon be cut down like the grass, and wither as the green herb.

Trust in the LORD, and do good; (so) shalt thou dwell in the land, and verily thou shalt be fed.

Delight thyself also in the LORD; and he shall give thee the desires of thine heart.

Commit thy way unto the LORD; trust also in him; and he shall bring (it) to pass.

And he shall bring forth thy righteousness as the light, and thy judgment as the noonday.

Rest in the LORD, and wait patiently for him: fret not thyself because of him who prospereth in his way, because of the man who bringeth wicked devices to pass.

Psalms 37:1-7

Fear thou not; for I (am) with thee: be not dismayed; for I (am) thy God: I will strengthen thee; yea, I will help thee; yea, I will uphold thee with the right hand of my righteousness.

Behold, all they that were incensed against thee shall be ashamed and confounded: they shall be as nothing; and they that strive with thee shall perish.

Isaiah 41:10, 11

[(A Psalm) of David.] The LORD (is) my light and my salvation; whom shall I fear? the LORD (is) the strength of my life; of whom shall I be afraid?

When the wicked, (even) mine enemies and my foes, came upon me to eat up my flesh, they stumbled and fell.

Though an host should encamp against me, my heart shall not fear: though war should rise against me, in this (will) I (be) confident.

One (thing) have I desired of the LORD, that will I seek after; that I may dwell in the house of the LORD all the days of my life, to behold the beauty of the LORD, and to inquire in his temple.

For in the time of trouble he shall hide me in his pavilion: in the secret of his tabernacle shall he hide me; he shall set me up upon a rock.

Psalms 27:1-5

Wait on the LORD: be of good courage, and he shall strengthen thine heart: wait, I say, on the LORD.

Psalms 27:14

[(A Psalm) of David.] The LORD (is) my sheperd; I shall not want.

He maketh me to lie down in green pastures: he leadeth me beside the still waters.

He restoreth my soul: he leadeth me in the paths of righteousness for his name's sake.

Yea, though I walk through the valley of the shadow of death, I will fear no evil: for thou (art) with me; thy rod and thy staff they comfort me.

Thou preparest a table before me in the presence of mine enemies: thou anointest my head with oil; my cup runneth over.

Surely goodness and mercy shall follow me all the days of my life: and I will dwell in the house of the LORD for ever.

Psalms 23:1-6

What time I am afraid, I will trust in thee.

In God I will praise his word, in God I have put my trust; I will not fear what flesh can do unto me.

Psalms 56:3, 4

Have not I commanded thee? Be strong and of a good courage; be not afraid, neither be thou dismayed: for the LORD thy God (is) with thee whithersoever thou goest.

Joshua 1:9

(He that is) slow to anger (is) better than the mighty; and he that ruleth his spirit than he that taketh a city.

Proverbs 16:32

Biblical Structures
For Your Business...

Administration & Organization

And he called (unto him) the twelve, and began to send them forth by two and two; and gave them power over unclean spirits;

And commanded them that they should take nothing for (their) journey, save a staff only; no scrip, no bread, no money in (their) purse:

But (be) shod with sandals; and not put on two coats.

And he said unto them, In what place soever ye enter into an house, there abide till ye depart from that place.

And whosoever shall not receive you, nor hear you, when ye depart thence, shake off the dust under your feet for a testimony against them. Verily I say unto you, It shall be more tolerable for Sodom and Gomorrha in the day of judgment, than for that city.

And they went out, and preached that men should repent.

And they cast out many devils, and anointed with oil many that were sick, and healed (them).

Mark 6:7-13

And the LORD spake unto Moses in the wilderness of Sinai, in the tabernacle of the congregation, on the first (day) of the second month, in the second year after they were come out of the land of Egypt, saying,

Take ye the sum of all the congregation of the children of Israel, after their families, by the house of their fathers, with the number of (their) names, every male by their polls;

From twenty years old and upward, all that are able to go forth to war in Israel: thou and Aaron shall number them by their armies.

And with you there shall be a man of every tribe; every one head of the house of his fathers.

Numbers 1:1-4

When the righteous are in authority, the people rejoice: but when the wicked beareth rule, the people mourn.

Proverbs 29:2

And it came to pass on the morrow, that Moses sat to judge the people: and the people stood by Moses from the morning unto the evening.

And when Moses' father in law saw all that he did to the people, he said, What (is) this thing that thou doest to the people? why sittest thou thyself alone, and all the people stand by thee from morning unto even?

And Moses said unto his father in law, Because the people come unto me to inquire of God:

When they have a matter, they come unto me; and I judge between one and another, and I do make (them) know the statutes of God, and his laws.

And Moses' father in law said unto him, The thing that thou doest (is) not good.

Thou wilt surely wear away, both thou, and this people that (is) with thee: for this thing (is) too heavy for thee; thou are not able to perform it thyself alone.

Hearken now unto my voice, I will give thee counsel, and God shall be with thee: Be thou for the people to God-ward, that thou mayest bring the causes unto God:

And thou shalt teach them ordinances and laws, and shalt shew them the way wherein they must walk, and the work that they must do.

Moreover thou shalt provide out of all the people able men, such as fear God, men of truth, hating covetousness; and place (such) over them, (to be) rulers of thousands, (and) rulers of hundreds, rulers of fifties, and rulers of tens:

And let them judge the people at all seasons: and it shall be, (that) every great matter they shall bring unto thee, but every small matter they shall judge: so shall it be easier for thyself, and they shall bear (the burden) with thee.

If thou shalt do this thing, and God command thee (so), then thou shalt be able to endure, and all this people shall also go to their place in peace.

So Moses hearkened to the voice of his father in law, and did all that he had said.

And Moses chose able men out of all Israel, and made them heads over the people, rulers of thousands, rulers of hundreds, rulers of fifties, and rulers of tens.

And they judged the people at all seasons: the hard causes they brought unto Moses, but every small matter they judged themselves.

And Moses let his father in law depart; and he went his way into his own land.

Exodus 18:13-27

And he called his ten servants, and delivered them ten pounds, and said unto them, Occupy till I come.

And it came to pass, that when he was returned, having received the kingdom, then he commanded these servants to be called unto him, to whom he had given the money, that he might know how much every man had gained by trading.

Then came the first, saying, Lord, thy pound hath gained ten pounds.

And he said unto him, Well, thou good servant: because thou hast been faithful in a very little, have thou authority over ten cities.

And the second came, saying, Lord, thy pound hath gained five pounds.

And he said likewise to him, Be thou also over five cities.

Luke 19:13, 15-19

And the Lord said, Who then is that faithful and wise steward, whom (his) lord shall make ruler over his household, to give (them their) portion of meat in due season?

Blessed (is) that servant, whom his lord when he cometh shall find so doing.

Of a truth I say unto you, that he will make him ruler over all that he hath.

Luke 12:42-44

And the Lord gave Solomon wisdom, as he promised him: and there was peace between Hiram and Solomon; and they two made a league together.

And king Solomon raised a levy out of all Israel; and the levy was thirty thousand men.

And he sent them to Lebanon, ten thousand a month by courses: a month they were in Lebanon, (and) two months at home: and Adoniram (was) over the levy.

And Solomon had threescore and ten thousand that bare burdens, and fourscore thousand hewers in the mountains;

Beside the chief of Solomon's officers which (were) over the work, three thousand and three hundred, which ruled over the people that wrought in the work.

And Solomon's builders and Hiram's builders did hew them, and the stonesquarers: so they prepared timber and stones to build the house.

I Kings 5:12-16, 18

Management Of People & Resources

Let every soul be subject unto the higher powers. For there is no power but of God: the powers that be are ordained of God.

Whosoever therefore resisteth the power, resisteth the ordinance of God: and they that resist shall receive to themselves damnation.

For rulers are not a terror to good works, but to the evil. Wilt thou then not be afraid of the power? do that which is good, and thou shalt have praise of the same:

For he is the minister of God to thee for good. But if thou do that which is evil, be afraid; for he beareth not the sword in vain: for he is the minister of God, a revenger to (execute) wrath upon him that doeth evil.

Wherefore (ye) must needs be subject, not only for wrath, but also for conscience sake.

For for this cause pay ye tribute also: for they are God's ministers, attending continually upon this very thing.

Render therefore to all their dues: tribute to whom tribute (is due); custom to whom custom; fear to whom fear; honour to whom honour.

Romans 13:1-7

He that is faithful in that which is least is faithful also in much: and he that is unjust in the least is unjust also in much.

If therefore ye have not been faithful in the unrighteous mammon, who will commit to your trust the true (riches)?

And if ye have not been faithful in that which is another man's, who shall give you that which is your own?

Luke 16:10-12

For (the kingdom of heaven is) as a man travelling into a far country, (who) called his own servants, and delivered unto them his goods.

And unto one he gave five talents, to another two, and to another one; to every man according to his several ability; and straightway took his journey.

Then he that had received the five talents went and traded with the same, and made (them) other five talents.

And likewise he that (had received) two, he also gained other two.

But he that had received one went and digged in the earth, and hid his lord's money.

After a long time the lord of those servants cometh, and reckoneth with them.

And so he that had received five talents came and brought other five talents, saying, Lord, thou deliveredst unto me five talents: behold, I have gained beside them five talents more.

His lord said unto him, Well done, (thou) good and faithful servant: thou has been faithful over a few things, I will make thee ruler over many things: enter thou into the joy of thy lord.

He also that had received two talents came and said, Lord, thou deliveredst unto me two talents: behold, I have gained two other talents beside them.

His lord said unto him, Well done, good and faithful servant; thou hast been faithful over a few things, I will make thee ruler over many things: enter thou into the joy of thy lord.

Matthew 25:14-23

And it came to pass, that when the Jews which dwelt by them came, they said unto us ten times, From all places whence ye shall return unto us (they will be upon you).

Therefore set I in the lower places behind the wall, (and) on the higher places, I even set the people after their families with their swords, their spears, and their bows.

And I looked, and rose up, and said unto the nobles, and to the rulers, and to the rest of the people, Be not ye afraid of them: remember the Lord, (which is) great and terrible, and fight for your brethren, your sons, and your daughters, your wives, and your houses.

And it came to pass, when our enemies heard that it was known unto us, and God had brought their counsel to nought, that we returned all of us to the wall, every one unto his work.

And it came to pass from that time forth, (that) the half of my servants wrought in the work, and the other half of them held both the spears, the shields, and the bows, and the habergeons; and the rulers (were) behind all the house of Judah.

They which builded on the wall, and they that bare burdens, with those that laded, (every one) with one of his hands wrought in the work, and with the other (hand) held a weapon.

For the builders, every one had his sword girded by his side, and (so) builded. And he that sounded the trumpet (was) by me.

And I said unto the nobles, and to the rulers, and to the rest of the people, The work (is) great and large, and we are separated upon the wall, one far from another.

In what place (therefore) ye hear the sound of the trumpet, resort ye thither unto us: our God shall fight for us.

So we laboured in the work: and half of them held the spears from the rising of the morning till the stars appeared.

Likewise at the same time said I unto the people, Let every one with his servant lodge within Jerusalem, that in the night they may be a guard to us, and labour on the day.

So neither I, nor my brethren, nor my servants, nor the men of the guard which followed me, none of us put off our clothes, (saving that) every one put them off for washing.

Nehemiah 4:12-23

Make thee an ark of gopher wood; rooms shalt thou make in the ark, and shalt pitch it within and without with pitch.

And this (is the fashion) which thou shalt make it (of): The length of the ark (shall be) three hundred cubits, the breadth of it fifty cubits, and the height of it thirty cubits.

A window shalt thou make to the ark, and in a cubit shalt thou finish it above; and the door of the ark shalt thou set in the side thereof; (with) lower, second, and third (stories) shalt thou make it.

And, behold, I, even I, do bring a flood of waters upon the earth, to destroy all flesh, wherein (is) the breath of life, from under heaven; (and) every thing that (is) in the earth shall die.

But with thee will I establish my covenant; and thou shalt come into the ark, thou, and thy sons, and thy wife, and thy sons' wives with thee.

And of every living thing of all flesh, two of every (sort) shalt thou bring into the ark, to keep (them) alive with thee; they shall be male and female.

Of fowls after their kind, and of cattle after their kind, of every creeping thing of the earth after his kind, two of every (sort) shall come unto thee, to keep (them) alive.

And take thou unto thee of all food that is eaten, and thou shalt gather (it) to thee; and it shall be for food for thee, and for them.

Thus did Noah; according to all that God commanded him, so did he.

Genesis 6:14-22

And the LORD was with Joseph, and he was a prosperous man; and he was in the house of his master the Egyptian.

And his master saw that the LORD (was) with him, and that the LORD made all that he did to prosper in his hand.

And Joseph found grace in his sight, and he served him: and he made him overseer over his house, and all (that) he had he put into his hand.

And it came to pass from the time (that) he had made him overseer in his house, and over all that he had, that the LORD blessed the Egyptian's house for Joseph's sake; and the blessing of the LORD was upon all that he had in the house, and in the field.

And he left all that he had in Joseph's hand; and he knew not ought he had, save the bread which he did eat. And Joseph was (a) goodly (person), and well favoured.

Genesis 39:2-6

But the LORD was with Joseph, and shewed him mercy, and gave him favour in the sight of the keeper of the prison.

And the keeper of the prison committed to Joseph's hand all the prisoners that (were) in the prison; and whatsoever they did there, he was the doer (of it).

The keeper of the prison looked not to any thing (that was) under his hand; because the LORD was with him, and (that) which he did, the LORD made (it) to prosper.

Genesis 39:21-23

And the thing was good in the eyes of Pharaoh, and in the eyes of all his servants.

And Pharaoh said unto his servants, Can we find (such a one) as this (is), a man in whom the spirit of God (is)?

And Pharaoh said unto Joseph, Forasmuch as God hath shewed thee all this, (there is) none so discreet and wise as thou (art):

Thou shalt be over my house, and according unto thy word shall all my people be ruled: only in the throne will I be greater than thou.

And Pharoah said unto Joseph, See, I have set thee over all the land of Egypt.

And Pharaoh took off his ring from his hand, and put it upon Joseph's hand, and arrayed him in vestures of fine linen, and put a gold chain about his neck;

And he made him to ride in the second chariot which he had; and they cried before him, Bow the knee: and he made him (ruler) over all the land of Egypt.

Genesis 41:37-43

And Joseph bought all the land of Egypt for Pharaoh; for the Egyptians sold every man his field, because the famine prevailed over them: so the land became Pharaoh's.

And as for the people, he removed them to cities from (one) end of the borders of Egypt even to the (other) end thereof.

Only the land of the priests bought he not; for the priests had a portion (assigned them) of Pharaoh, and did eat their portion which Pharaoh gave them: wherefore they sold not their lands.

Then Joseph said unto the people, Behold, I have bought you this day and your land for Pharaoh: lo, (here is) seed for you, and ye shall sow the land.

And it shall come to pass in the increase, that ye shall give the fifth (part) unto Pharaoh, and four parts shall be your own, for seed of the field, and for your food, and for them of your households, and for food for your little ones.

And they said, Thou hast saved our lives: let us find grace in the sight of my lord, and we will be Pharaoh's servants.

And Joseph made it a law over the land of Egypt unto this day, (that) Pharoah should have the fifth (part); except the land of the priests only, (which) became not Pharaoh's.

And Israel dwelt in the land of Egypt, in the country of Goshen; and they had possessions therein, and grew, and multiplied exceedingly.

Genesis 47:20-27

Now when he was in Jerusalem at the passover, in the feast (day), many believed in his name, when they saw the miracles which he did.

But Jesus did not commit himself unto them, because he knew all (men),

And needed not that any should testify of man: for he knew what was in man.

John 2:23-25

Boast not thyself of to morrow; for thou knowest not what a day may bring forth.

Proverbs 27:1

Training & Development

A wise (man) will hear, and will increase learning; and a man of understanding shall attain unto wise counsels:

Proverbs 1:5

The fear of the Lord (is) the beginning of knowledge: (but) fools despise wisdom and instruction.

Proverbs 1:7

My son, hear the instruction of thy father, and forsake not the law of thy mother:
For they (shall be) an ornament of grace unto thy head, and chains about thy neck.

Proverbs 1:8, 9

Turn you at my reproof: behold, I will pour out my spirit unto you, I will make known my words unto you.

Proverbs 1:23

And thou shalt teach them diligently unto thy children, and shalt talk of them when thou sittest in thine house, and when thou walkest by the way, and when thou liest down, and when thou risest up.

Deuteronomy 6:7

Train up a child in the way he should go: and when he is old, he will not depart from it.

Proverbs 22:6

And, ye fathers, provoke not your children to wrath: but bring them up in the nurture and admonition of the Lord.

Ephesians 6:4

The rod and reproof give wisdom: but a child left (to himself) bringeth his mother to shame.

Proverbs 29:15

Come, ye children, hearken unto me: I will teach you the fear of the LORD.

Psalms 34:11

And the child Samuel grew on, and was in favour both with the LORD, and also with men.

I Samuel 2:26

Now the days of David drew nigh that he should die; and he charged Solomon his son, saying,

I go the way of all the earth: be thou strong therefore, and shew thyself a man;

And keep the charge of the LORD thy God, to walk in his ways, to keep his statutes, and his commandments, and his judgments, and his testimonies, as it is written in the law of Moses, that thou mayest prosper in all that thou doest, and whithersoever thou turnest thyself:

That the LORD may continue his word which he spake concerning me, saying, If thy children take heed to their way, to walk before me in truth with all their heart and with all their soul, there shall not fail thee (said he) a man on the throne of Israel.

I Kings 2:1-4

And Jesus increased in wisdom and stature, and in favour with God and man.

Luke 2:52

And they went into Capernaum; and straightway on the sabbath day he entered into the synagogue, and taught.

And they were astonished at his doctrine: for he taught them as one that had authority, and not as the scribes.

Mark 1:21, 22

And he began again to teach by the sea side: and there was gathered unto him a great multitude, so that he entered into a ship and sat in the sea; and the whole multitude was by the sea on the land.

Mark 4:1

And with many such parables spake he the word unto them, as they were able to hear (it).

But without a parable spake he not unto them: and when they were alone, he expounded all things to his disciples.

Mark 4:33, 34

And Jesus, when he came out, saw much people, and was moved with compassion toward them, because they were as sheep not having a shepherd: and he began to teach them many things.

Mark 6:34

My son, if thou wilt receive my words, and hide my commandments with thee;

So that thou incline thine ear unto wisdom, (and) apply thine heart to understanding;

Yea, if thou criest after knowledge, (and) liftest up thy voice for understanding;

If thou seekest her as silver, and searchest for her as (for) hid treasures;

Then shalt thou understand the fear of the LORD, and find the knowledge of God.

Proverbs 2:1-5

I have taught thee in the way of wisdom; I have led thee in right paths.

Proverbs 4:11

When thou goest, thy steps shall not be straitened; and when thou runnest, thou shalt not stumble.

Proverbs 4:12

Take fast hold of instruction; let (her) not go; keep her; for she (is) thy life.

Proverbs 4:13

For the ways of man (are) before the eyes of the LORD, and he pondereth all his goings.

Proverbs 5:21

His own iniquities shall take the wicked himself, and he shall be holden with the cords of his sins.

Proverbs 5:22

He shall die without instruction; and in the greatness of his folly he shall go astray.

Proverbs 5:23

Receive my instruction, and not silver; and knowledge rather than choice gold.

Proverbs 8:10

Hear instruction, and be wise, and refuse it not.

Proverbs 8:33

Give (instruction) to a wise (man), and he will be yet wiser; teach a just (man), and he will increase in learning.

Proverbs 9:9

He (is in) the way of life that keepeth instruction: but he that refuseth reproof erreth.

Proverbs 10:17

Whoso loveth instruction loveth knowledge: but he that hateth reproof (is) brutish.

Proverbs 12:1

Delegation Of Authority & Responsibility

The soul that sinneth, it shall die. The son shall not bear the iniquity of the father, neither shall the father bear the iniquity of the son: the righteousness of the righteous shall be upon him, and the wickedness of the wicked shall be upon him.

Ezekiel 18:20

Therefore I will judge you, O house of Israel, every one according to his ways, saith the Lord GOD. Repent, and turn (yourselves) from all your transgressions; so iniquity shall not be your ruin.

Ezekiel 18:30

For by thy words thou shalt be justified, and by thy words thou shalt be condemned.

Matthew 12:37

For every man shall bear his own burden.

Galatians 6:5

Now he that planteth and he that watereth are one: and every man shall receive his own reward according to his own labour.

I Corinthians 3:8

Every man's work shall be made manifest: for the day shall declare it, because it shall be revealed by fire; and the fire shall try every man's work of what sort it is.

If any man's work abide which he hath built thereupon, he shall receive a reward.

I Corinthians 3:13, 14

But unto every one of us is given grace according to the measure of the gift of Christ.

Ephesians 4:7

Charge them that are rich in this world, that they be not highminded, not trust in uncertain riches, but in the living God, who giveth us richly all things to enjoy;

That they do good, that they be rich in good works, ready to distribute, willing to communicate;

Laying up in store for themselves a good foundation against the time to come, that they may lay hold on eternal life.

O Timothy, keep that which is committed to thy trust, avoiding profane (and) vain babblings, and oppositions of science falsely so called:

Which some professing have erred concerning the faith. Grace (be) with thee. Amen.

I Timothy 6:17-21

But ye shall receive power, after that the Holy Ghost is come upon you: and ye shall be witnesses unto me both in Jerusalem, and in all Judaea, and in Samaria, and unto the uttermost part of the earth.

Acts 1:8

And Jesus came and spake unto them, saying, All power is given unto me in heaven and in earth.

Go ye therefore, and teach all nations, baptizing them in the name of the Father, and of the Son, and of the Holy Ghost:

Teaching them to observe all things whatsoever I have commanded you: and, lo, I am with you alway, (even) unto the end of the world. Amen.

Matthew 28:18-20

If thou be wise, thou shalt be wise for thyself: but if thou scornest, thou alone shalt bear (it).

Proverbs 9:12

But every one shall die for his own iniquity: every man that eateth the sour grape, his teeth shall be set on edge.

Jeremiah 31:30

And the LORD said, I have surely seen the affliction of my people which (are) in Egypt, and have heard their cry by reason of their taskmasters; for I know their sorrows;

Now therefore, behold, the cry of the children of Israel is come unto me: and I have also seen the oppression wherewith the Egyptians oppress them.

Come now therefore, and I will send thee unto Pharaoh, that thou mayest bring forth my people the children of Israel out of Egypt.

Exodus 3:7, 9, 10

And the LORD said unto Moses, Wherefore criest thou unto me? speak unto the children of Israel, that they go forward:

But lift thou up thy rod, and stretch out thine hand over the sea, and divide it: and the children of Israel shall go on dry (ground) through the midst of the sea.

Exodus 14:15, 16

And he cried unto the LORD; and the LORD shewed him a tree, (which) when he had cast into the waters, the waters were made sweet: there he made for them a statute and an ordinance, and there he proved them,

And said, If thou wilt diligently hearken to the voice of the LORD thy God, and wilt do that which is right in his sight, and wilt give ear to his commandments, and keep all his statutes, I will put none of these diseases upon thee, which I have brought upon the Egyptians: for I (am) the LORD that healeth thee.

Exodus 15:25, 26

And the LORD God planted a garden eastward in Eden; and there he put the man whom he had formed.

And the LORD God took the man, and put him into the garden of Eden to dress it and to keep it.

Genesis 2:8, 15

Now after the death of Moses the servant of the LORD it came to pass, that the LORD spake unto Joshua the son of Nun, Moses' minister, saying,

Moses my servant is dead; now therefore arise, go over this Jordan, thou, and all this people, unto the land which I do give to them, (even) to the children of Israel.

Every place that the sole of your foot shall tread upon, that have I given unto you, as I said unto Moses.

From the wilderness and this Lebanon even unto the great river, the river Euphrates, all the land of the Hittites, and unto the great sea toward the going down of the sun, shall be your coast.

There shall not any man be able to stand before thee all the days of thy life: as I was with Moses, (so) I will be with thee: I will not fail thee, nor forsake thee.

Be strong and of a good courage: for unto this people shalt thou divide for an inheritance the land, which I sware unto their fathers to give them.

Only be thou strong and very courageous, that thou mayest observe to do according to all the law, which Moses my servant commanded thee: turn not from it (to) the right hand or (to) the left, that thou mayest prosper withersoever thou goest.

This book of the law shall not depart out of thy mouth; but thou shalt meditate therein day and night, that thou mayest observe to do according to all that is written therein: for then thou shalt make thy way prosperous, and then thou shalt have good success.

Have not I commanded thee? Be strong and of a good courage; be not afraid, neither be thou dismayed: for the LORD thy God (is) with thee whithersoever thou goest.

Joshua 1:1-9

(To the chief Musician upon Gittith, A Psalm of David.) O LORD our Lord, how excellent (is) thy name in all the earth! who has set thy glory above the heavens.

Out of the mouths of babes and sucklings hast thou ordained strength because of thine enemies, that thou mightest still the enemy and the avenger.

When I consider thy heavens, the work of thy fingers, the moon and the stars, which thou hast ordained;

What is man, that thou art mindful of him? and the son of man, that thou visitest him?

For thou hast made him a little lower than the angels, and hast crowned him with glory and honour.

Thou madest him to have dominion over the works of thy hands; thou hast put all (things) under his feet:

All sheep and oxen, yea, and the beasts of the field;

The fowl of the air, and the fish of the sea, (and whatsoever) passeth through the paths of the seas.

O LORD our Lord, how excellent (is) thy name in all the earth!

Psalms 8:1-9

Team Spirit

Brethren, if a man be overtaken in a fault, ye which are spiritual, restore such an one in the spirit of meekness; considering thyself, lest thou also be tempted.

Bear ye one another's burdens, and so fulfill the law of Christ.

Galatians 6:1, 2

Two (are) better than one; because they have a good reward for their labour.

For if they fall, the one will lift up his fellow: but woe to him (that is) alone when he falleth; for (he hath) not another to help him up.

Again, if two lie together, then they have heat: but how can one be warm (alone)?

And if one prevail against him, two shall withstand him; and a threefold cord is not quickly broken.

Ecclesiastes 4:9-12

And Jesus knew their thoughts, and said unto them, Every kingdom divided against itself is brought to desolation; and every city or house divided against itself shall not stand:

Matthew 12:25

He that is not with me is against me; and he that gathereth not with me scattereth abroad.

Matthew 12:30

(Let) love be without dissimulation. Abhor that which is evil; cleave to that which is good.

(Be) kindly affectioned one to another with brotherly love; in honour preferring one another;

Not slothful in business; fervent in spirit; serving the Lord;

Rejoicing in hope; patient in tribulation; continuing instant in prayer;

Distributing to the necessity of saints; given to hospitality.

Romans 12:9-13

(A Song of degrees of David.) Behold, how good and how pleasant (it is) for brethren to dwell together in unity!

Psalms 133:1

Cast out the scorner, and contention shall go out; yea, strife and reproach shall cease.

Proverbs 22:10

Finally, (be ye) all of one mind, having compassion one of another, love as brethren, (be) pitiful, (be) courteous:

Not rendering evil for evil, or railing for railing: but contrariwise blessing; knowing that ye are thereunto called, that ye should inherit a blessing.

I Peter 3:8, 9

God (is) faithful, by whom ye were called unto the fellowship of his Son Jesus Christ our Lord.

Now I beseech you, brethren, by the name of our Lord Jesus Christ, that ye all speak the same thing, and (that) there be no divisions among you; but (that) ye be perfectly joined together in the same mind and in the same judgment.

I Corinthians 1:9, 10

Now therefore ye are no more strangers and foreigners, but fellowcitizens with the saints, and of the household of God;

And are built upon the foundation of the apostles and prophets, Jesus Christ himself being the chief corner (stone);

In whom all the building fitly framed together groweth unto an holy temple in the Lord:

In whom ye also are builded together for an habitation of God through the Spirit.

Ephesians 2:19-22

Ye call me Master and Lord; and ye say well; for (so) I am.

If I then, (your) Lord and Master, have washed your feet; ye also ought to wash one another's feet.

John 13:13, 14

Bless them which persecute you: bless, and curse not.

Rejoice with them that do rejoice, and weep with them that weep.

(Be) of the same mind one toward another. Mind not high things, but condescend to men of low estate. Be not wise in your own conceits.

Recompense to no man evil for evil. Provide things honest in the sight of all men.

If it be possible, as much as lieth in you, live peaceably with all men.

Dearly beloved, avenge not yourselves, but (rather) give place unto wrath: for it is written, Vengeance (is) mine; I will repay, saith the Lord.

Therefore if thine enemy hunger, feed him; if he thirst, give him drink: for in so doing thou shalt heap coals of fire on his head.

Romans 12:14-20

For where two or three are gathered together in my name, there am I in the midst of them.

Matthew 18:20

While he spake these things unto them, behold, there came a certain ruler, and worshipped him, saying, My daughter is even now dead: but come and lay thy hand upon her, and she shall live.

And Jesus arose, and followed him, and (so did) his disciples.

Matthew 9:18, 19

But if ye bite and devour one another, take heed that ye be not consumed one of another.

Galatians 5:15

Let us not be desirous of vain glory, provoking one another, envying one another.

Galatians 5:26

Wherefore comfort yourselves together, and edify one another, even as also ye do.

And we beseech you, brethren, to know them which labour among you, and are over you in the Lord, and admonish you;

And to esteem them very highly in love for their work's sake. (And) be at peace among yourselves.

I Thessalonians 5:11-13

For I have given you an example, that ye should do as I have done to you.

Verily, verily, I say unto you, The servant is not greater than his lord; neither he that is sent greater than he that sent him.

If ye know these things, happy are ye if ye do them.

John 13:15-17

Time Management

Go to now, ye that say, To day or to morrow we will go into such a city, and continue there a year, and buy and sell, and get gain:

Whereas ye know not what (shall be) on the morrow. For what (is) your life? It is even a vapour, that appeareth for a little time, and then vanisheth away.

For that ye (ought) to say, If the Lord will, we shall live, and do this, or that.

But now ye rejoice in your boastings: all such rejoicing is evil.

Therefore to him that knoweth to do good, and doeth (it) not, to him it is sin.

James 4:13-17

Go to the ant, thou sluggard; consider her ways, and be wise:

Which having no guide, overseer, or ruler,

Provideth her meat in the summer, (and) gathereth her food in the harvest.

How long wilt thou sleep, O sluggard? when wilt thou arise out of thy sleep?

(Yet) a little sleep, a little slumber, a little folding of the hands to sleep:

So shall thy poverty come as one that travelleth, and thy want as an armed man.

Proverbs 6:6-11

Now it came to pass, as they went, that he entered into a certain village: and a certain woman named Martha received him into her house.

And she had a sister called Mary, which also sat at Jesus' feet, and heard his word.

But Martha was cumbered about much serving, and came to him, and said, Lord, dost thou not care that my sister hath left me to serve alone? bid her therefore that she help me.

And Jesus answered and said unto her, Martha, Martha, thou art careful and troubled about many things:

But one thing is needful: and Mary hath chosen that good part, which shall not be taken away from her.

Luke 10:38-42

And at even, when the sun did set, they brought unto him all that were diseased, and them that were possessed with devils.

And all the city was gathered together at the door.

And he healed many that were sick of divers diseases, and cast out many devils; and suffered not the devils to speak, because they knew him.

And in the morning, rising up a great while before day, he went out, and departed into a solitary place, and there prayed.

And Simon and they that were with him followed after him.

And when they had found him, they said unto him, All (men) seek for thee.

And he said unto them, Let us go into the next towns, that I may preach there also: for therefore came I forth.

Mark 1:32-38

I must work the works of him that sent me, while it is day: the night cometh, when no man can work.

John 9:4

I said in mine heart, God shall judge the righteous and the wicked: for (there is) a time there for every purpose and for every work.

Ecclesiastes 3:17

And it came to pass, that, as they went in the way, a certain (man) said unto him, Lord, I will follow thee withersoever thou goest.

And Jesus said unto him, Foxes have holes, and birds of the air (have) nests; but the Son of man hath not where to lay (his) head.

And he said unto another, Follow me. But he said, Lord, suffer me first to go and bury my father.

Jesus said unto him, Let the dead bury their dead: but go thou and preach the kingdom of God.

And another also said, Lord, I will follow thee; but let me first go bid them farewell, which are at home at my house.

And Jesus said unto him, No man, having put his hand to the plough, and looking back, is fit for the kingdom of God.

Luke 9:57-62

He that gathereth in summer (is) a wise son: (but) he that sleepeth in harvest (is) a son that causeth shame.

Proverbs 10:5

Love not sleep, lest thou come to poverty;
open thine eyes, (and) thou shalt be satisfied with
bread.

Proverbs 20:13

Boast not thyself of to morrow; for thou
knowest not what a day may bring forth.

Proverbs 27:1

I (counsel thee) to keep the king's commandment, and (that) in regard of the oath of God.

Be not hasty to go out of his sight: stand not
in an evil thing; for he doeth whatsoever pleaseth
him.

Where the word of a king (is, there is) power:
and who may say unto him, What doest thou?

Whoso keepeth the commandment shall feel
no evil thing: and a wise man's heart discerneth both
time and judgment.

Because to every purpose there is time and
judgment, therefore the misery of man (is) great
upon him.

For he knoweth not that which shall be: for
who can tell him when it shall be?

Ecclesiastes 8:2-7

Biblical Growth For Your Business...

Productivity

Honour the LORD with thy substance, and with the firstfruits of all thine increase:

So shall thy barns be filled with plenty, and thy presses shall burst out with new wine.

Proverbs 3:9, 10

Apply thine heart unto instruction, and thine ears to the words of knowledge.

Proverbs 23:12

Seest thou a man diligent in his business? he shall stand before kings; he shall not stand before mean (men).

Proverbs 22:29

A wise man (is) strong; yea, a man of knowledge increaseth strength.

Proverbs 24:5

For by wise counsel thou shalt make thy war: and in multitude of counsellors (there is) safety.

Proverbs 24:6

Prepare thy work without, and make it fit for thyself in the field; and afterwards build thine house.

Proverbs 24:27

(There is) nothing better for a man, (than) that he should eat and drink, and (that) he should make his soul enjoy good in his labour. This also I saw, that it (was) from the hand of God.

Ecclesiastes 2:24

Wherefore I perceive that (there is) nothing better, than that a man should rejoice in his own works; for that (is) his portion: for who shall bring him to see what shall be after him?

Ecclesiastes 3:22

When I applied mine heart to know wisdom, and to see the business that is done upon the earth: (for also (there is that) neither day nor night seeth sleep with his eyes:)

Then I beheld all the work of God, that a man cannot find out the work that is done under the sun: because though a man labour to seek (it) out, yet he shall not find (it): yea farther: though a wise (man) think to know (it), yet shall he not be able to find (it).

Ecclesiastes 8:16, 17

Go thy way, eat thy bread with joy, and drink thy wine with a merry heart; for God now accepteth thy works.

Let thy garments be always white; and let thy head lack no ointment.

Live joyfully with the wife whom thou lovest all the days of the life of thy vanity, which he hath given thee under the sun, all the days of thy vanity: for that (is) thy portion in (this) life, and in thy labour which thou takest under the sun.

Whatsoever they hand findeth to do, do (it) with thy might; for (there is) no work, nor device, nor knowledge, nor wisdom, in the grave, whither thou goest.

Ecclesiastes 9:7-10

He that is faithful in that which is least is faithful also in much: and he that is unjust in the least is unjust also in much.

If therefore ye have not been faithful in the unrighteous mammon, who will commit to your trust the true (riches)?

And if ye have not been faithful in that which is another man's who shall give you that which is your own?

No servant can serve two masters: for either he will hate the one, and love the other; or else he will hold to the one, and despise the other. Ye cannot serve God and mammon.

Luke 16:10-13

But let every man prove his own work, and then shall he have rejoicing in himself alone, and not in another.

For every man shall bear his own burden.

Let him that is taught in the word communicate unto him that teacheth in all good things.

And let us not be weary in well doing: for in due season we shall reap, if we faint not.

Galatians 6:4-6, 9

Now he that planteth and he that watereth are one: and every man shall receive his own reward according to his own labour.

For we are labourers together with God: ye are God's husbandry, (ye are) God's building.

I Corinthians 3:8, 9

Ye have not chosen me, but I have chosen you, and ordained you, that ye should go and bring forth fruit, and (that) your fruit should remain: that whatsoever ye shall ask of the Father in my name, he may give it you.

These things I command you, that ye love one another.

John 15:16, 17

And whosoever doth not bear his cross, and come after me, cannot be my disciple.

For which of you, intending to build a tower, sitteth not down first, and counteth the cost, whether he have (sufficient) to finish (it)?

Lest haply, after he hath laid the foundation, and is not able to finish (it), all that behold (it) begin to mock him,

Saying, This man began to build, and was not able to finish.

So likewise, whosoever he be of you that forsaketh not all that he hath, he cannot be my disciple.

Luke 14:27-30, 33

Planning & Goal-Setting

A man's heart deviseth his way: but the Lord directeth his steps.

Proverbs 16:9

Let thine eyes look right on, and let thine eyelids look straight before thee.

Proverbs 4:25

Ponder the path of thy feet, and let all thy ways be established.

Proverbs 4:26

Shew me thy ways, O Lord; teach me thy paths.

Psalms 25:4

I will instruct thee and teach thee in the way which thou shalt go: I will guide thee with mine eye.

Psalms 32:8

Trust in the LORD with all thine heart; and lean not unto thine own understanding.

In all thy ways acknowledge him, and he shall direct thy paths.

Proverbs 3:5, 6

Hear counsel, and receive instruction, that thou mayest be wise in thy latter end.

Proverbs 19:20

(There are) many devices in a man's heart; nevertheless the counsel of the LORD, that shall stand.

Proverbs 19:21

And God looked upon the earth, and, behold, it was corrupt; for all flesh had corrupted his way upon the earth.

And God said unto Noah, The end of all flesh is come before me; for the earth is filled with violence through them; and, behold, I will destroy them with the earth.

Make thee an ark of gopher wood; rooms shalt thou make in the ark, and shalt pitch it within and without with pitch.

And this (is the fashion) which thou shalt make it (of): The length of the ark (shall be) three hundred cubits, the breadth of it fifty cubits, and the height of it thirty cubits.

A window shalt thou make to the ark, and in a cubit shalt thou finish it above; and the door of the ark shalt thou set in the side thereof; (with) lower, second, and third (stories) shalt thou make it.

And, behold, I, even I, do bring a flood of waters upon the earth, to destroy all flesh, wherein (is) the breath of life, from under heaven; (and) every thing that (is) in the earth shall die.

But with thee will I establish my covenant; and thou shalt come into the ark, thou, and thy sons, and thy wife, and thy sons' wives with thee.

And of every living thing of all flesh, two of every (sort) shalt thou bring into the ark, to keep (them) alive with thee; they shall be male and female.

Of fowls after their kind, and of cattle after their kind, of every creeping thing of the earth after his kind, two of every (sort) shall come unto thee, to keep (them) alive.

And take thou unto thee of all food that is eaten, and thou shalt gather (it) to thee; and it shall be for food for thee, and for them.

Thus did Noah; according to all that God commanded him, so did he.

Genesis 6:12-22

For which of you, intending to build a tower, sitteth not down first, and counteth the cost, whether he have (sufficient) to finish (it)?

Lest haply, after he hath laid the foundation, and is not able to finish (it), all that behold (it) begin to mock him,

Saying, This man began to build, and was not able to finish.

Or what king, going to make war against another king, sitteth not down first and consulteth whether he be able with ten thousand to meet him that cometh against him with twenty thousand?

Or else, while the other is yet a great way off, he sendeth an ambassage, and desireth conditions of peace.

Luke 14:28-32

Without counsel purposes are disappointed: but in the multitude of counsellors they are established.

Proverbs 15:22

(Every) purpose is established by counsel: and with good advice make war.

Proverbs 20:18

Counsel in the heart of man (is like) deep water; but a man of understanding will draw it out.

Proverbs 20:5

For by wise counsel thou shalt make thy war: and in multitude of counsellors (there is) safety.

Proverbs 24:6

The simple believeth every word: but the prudent (man) looketh well to his going.

Proverbs 14:15

Go not forth hastily to strive, lest (thou know not) what to do in the end thereof, when thy neighbour hath put thee to shame.

Proverbs 25:8

The steps of a (good) man are ordered by the LORD: and he delighteth in his way.

Psalms 37:23

Commitment To Quality & Value

And he spake this parable unto them saying, What man of you, having an hundred sheep, if he lose one of them, doth not leave the ninety and nine in the wilderness, and go after that which is lost, until he find it?

And when he hath found (it), he layeth (it) on his shoulders, rejoicing.

And when he cometh home, he calleth together (his) friends and neighbours, saying unto them, Rejoice with me; for I have found my sheep which was lost.

Luke 15:3-6

But let every man prove his own work, and then shall he have rejoicing in himself alone, and not in another.

Galatians 6:4

He must increase, but I (must) decrease.

John 3:30

For every man shall bear his own burden.

Galatians 6:5

Jesus answered and said unto her, Whosoever drinketh of this water shall thirst again:

But whosoever drinketh of the water that I shall give him shall never thirst; but the water that I shall give him shall be in him a well of water springing up into everlasting life.

John 4:13, 14

I, THEREFORE, the prisoner of the Lord, beseech you that ye walk worthy of the vocation wherewith ye are called,

With all lowliness and meekness, with longsuffering, forbearing one another in love;

Endeavouring to keep the unity of the Spirit in the bond of peace.

(There is) one body, and one Spirit, even as ye are called in one hope of your calling;

Ephesians 3:1-4

But Daniel purposed in his heart that he would not defile himself with the portion of the king's meat, nor with the wine which he drank: therefore he requested of the prince of the eunuchs that he might not defile himself.

Now God had brought Daniel into favour and tender love with the prince of the eunuchs.

And the prince of the eunuchs said unto Daniel, I fear my lord the king, who hath appointed your meat and your drink: for why should he see your faces worse liking than the children which (are) of your sort? then shall ye make (me) endanger my head to the king.

Then said Daniel to Melzar, whom the prince of the eunuchs had set over Daniel, Hananiah, Mishael, and Azariah,

Prove thy servants, I beseech thee, ten days; and let them give us pulse to eat, and water to drink.

Then let our countenances be looked upon before thee, and the countenance of the children that eat of the portion of the king's meat: and as thou seest, deal with thy servants.

So he consented to them in this matter, and proved them ten days.

And at the end of ten days their countenances appeared fairer and fatter in flesh than all the children which did eat the portion of the king's meat.

Thus Melzar took away the portion of their meat, and the wine that they should drink; and gave them pulse.

Daniel 1:8-16

And when they wanted wine, the mother of Jesus saith unto him, They have no wine.

Jesus saith unto them, Fill the waterpots with water. And they filled them up to the brim.

And he saith unto them, Draw out now, and bear unto the governor of the feast. And they bare (it).

When the ruler of the feast had tasted the water that was made wine, and knew not whence it was: (but the servants which drew the water knew;) the governor of the feast called the bridegroom,

And saith unto him, Every man at the beginning doth set forth good wine; and when men have well drunk, then that which is worse: (but) thou hast kept the good wine until now.

John 2:3, 7-10

Prosperity

This book of the law shall not depart out of thy mouth; but thou shalt meditate therein day and night, that thou mayest observe to do according to all that is written therein: for then thou shalt make thy way prosperous, and then thou shalt have good success.

Joshua 1:8

Let them shout for joy, and be glad, that favour my righteous cause: yea, let them say continually, Let the LORD be magnified, which hath pleasure in the prosperity of his servant.

Psalms 35:27

And Joseph was brought down to Egypt; and Potiphar, an officer of Pharaoh, captain of the guard, an Egyptian, bought him of the hands of the Ishmeelites, which had brought him down thither.

And the LORD was with Joseph, and he was a prosperous man; and he was in the house of his master the Egyptian.

And his master saw that the LORD (was) with him, and that the LORD made all that he did to prosper in his hand.

Genesis 39:1-3

Keep therefore the words of this covenant, and do them, that ye may prosper in all that ye do.

Deuteronomy 29:9

Then shalt thou prosper, if thou takest heed
to fulfil the statutes and judgments which the LORD
charged Moses with concerning Israel: be strong,
and of good courage; dread not, nor be dismayed.

I Chronicles 22:13

And he sought God in the days of Zechariah,
who had understanding in the visions of God: and
as long as he sought the LORD, God made him to
prosper.

II Chronicles 26:5

And thus did Hezekiah throughout all Judah,
and wrought (that which was) good and right and
truth before the LORD his God.

And in every work that he began in the service of the house of God, and in the law, and in the
commandents, to seek his God, he did (it) with all
his heart, and prospered.

II Chronicles 31:20, 21

Then answered I them, and said unto them,
The God of heaven, he will prosper us; therefore we
his servants will arise and build: but ye have no portion, nor right, nor memorial, in Jerusalem.

Nehemiah 2:20

And he shall be like a tree planted by the
rivers of water, that bringeth forth his fruit in his
season; his leaf also shall not wither; and whatsoever
he doeth shall prosper.

Psalms 1:3

Pray for the peace of Jerusalem: they shall prosper that love thee.

Psalms 122:6

Bring ye all the tithes into the storehouse, that there may be meat in mine house, and prove me now herewith, saith the LORD of hosts, if I will not open you the windows of heaven, and pour you out a blessing, that (there shall) not (be room) enough (to receive it).

Malachi 3:10

But seek ye first the kingdom of God, and his righteousness; and all these things shall be added unto you.

Matthew 6:33

And they rose early in the morning, and went forth into the wilderness of Tekoa: and as they went forth, Jehoshaphat stood and said, Hear me, O Judah, and ye inhabitants of Jerusalem; Believe in the LORD your God, so shall ye be established; believe his prophets, so shall ye prosper.

II Chronicles 20:20

And he spake a parable unto them, saying, The ground of a certain rich man brought forth plentifully:

And he thought within himself, saying, What shall I do, because I have no room where to bestow my fruits?

And he said, This will I do: I will pull down my barns, and build greater; and there will I bestow all my fruits and my goods.

And I will say to my soul, Soul, thou hast much goods laid up for many years; take thine ease, eat, drink, (and) be merry.

But God said unto him, (Thou) fool, this night thy soul shall be required of thee: then whose shall those things be, which thou hast provided?

So (is) he that layeth up treasure for himself, and is not rich toward God.

Luke 12:16-21

There was a certain rich man, which was clothed in purple and fine linen, and fared sumptuously every day:

And there was a certain beggar named Lazarus, which was laid at his gate, full of sores,

And desiring to be fed with the crumbs which fell from the rich man's table: moreover the dogs came and licked his sores.

And it came to pass, that the beggar died, and was carried by the angels into Abraham's bosom: the rich man also died, and was buried;

And in hell he lift up his eyes, being in torments, and seeth Abraham afar off, and Lazarus in his bosom.

And he cried and said, Father Abraham, have mercy on me, and send Lazarus, that he may dip the tip of his finger in water, and cool my tongue; for I am tormented in this flame.

But Abraham said, Son, remember that thou in thy lifetime receivedst thy good things, and likewise Lazarus evil things: but now he is comforted, and thou art tormented.

Luke 16:19-25

He that is faithful in that which is least is faithful also in much: and he that is unjust in the least is unjust also in much.

Luke 16:10

And when Jesus saw that he was very sorrowful, he said, How hardly shall they that have riches enter into the kingdom of God!
For it is easier for a camel to go through a needle's eye, than for a rich man to enter into the kingdom of God.

Luke 18:24, 25

Go to now, (ye) rich men, weep and howl for your miseries that shall come upon (you).
Your riches are corrupted, and your garments are motheaten.
Your gold and silver is cankered; and the rust of them shall be a witness against you, and shall eat your flesh as it were fire. Ye have heaped treasure together for the last days.

James 5:1-3

Then shall they call upon me, but I will not answer; they shall seek me early, but they shall not find me:

Proverbs 1:28

By humility (and) the fear of the LORD (are) riches, and honour, and life.

Proverbs 22:4

Every man also to whom God hath given riches and wealth, and hath given him power to eat thereof, and to take his portion, and to rejoice in his labour; this (is) the gift of God.

Ecclesiastes 5:19

In the day of prosperity be joyful, but in the day of adversity consider: God also hath set the one over against the other, to the end that man should find nothing after him.

Ecclesiastes 7:14

Sales

Whatsoever thy hand findeth to do, do it with thy might; for there is no work, nor device, nor knowledge, nor wisdom, in the grave, wither thou goest.

Ecclesiastes 9:10

Brethren, I count not myself to have apprehended: but this one thing I do, forgetting those things which are behind, and reaching forth unto those things which are before,

I press toward the mark for the prize of the high calling of God in Christ Jesus.

Philippians 3:13, 14

And he said unto them, Which of you shall have a friend, and shall go unto him at midnight, and say unto him, Friend, lend me three loaves;

For a friend of mine in his journey is come to me, and I have nothing to set before him?

And he from within shall answer and say, Trouble me not: the door is now shut, and my children are with me in bed; I cannot rise and give thee.

I say unto you, Though he will not rise and give him, because he is his friend, yet because of his importunity he will rise and give him as many as he needeth.

And I say unto you, Ask, and it shall be given you; seek, and ye shall find; knock, and it shall be opened unto you.

For every one that asketh receiveth; and he that seeketh findeth; and to him that knocketh it shall be opened.

Luke 11:5-10

Be not deceived; God is not mocked: for whatsoever a man soweth, that shall he also reap.

For he that soweth to his flesh shall of the flesh reap corruption; but he that soweth to the Spirit shall of the Spirit reap life everlasting.

And let us not be weary in well doing: for in due season we shall reap, if we faint not.

As we have therefore opportunity, let us do good unto all (men), especially unto them who are of the household of faith.

Galatians 6:7-10

Then he said, I pray thee therefore, father, that thou wouldest send him to my father's house:

For I have five brethren; that he may testify unto them, lest they also come into this place of torment.

Luke 16:27, 28

Ye are the light of the world. A city that is set on an hill cannot be hid.

Neither do men light a candle, and put it under a bushel, but on a candlestick; and it giveth light unto all that are in the house.

Let your light so shine before men, that they may see your good works, and glorify your Father which is in heaven.

Matthew 5:14-16

Say not ye, There are yet four months, and (then) cometh harvest? behold, I say unto you, Lift up your eyes, and look on the fields; for they are white already to harvest.

And he that reapeth receiveth wages, and gathereth fruit unto life eternal: that both he that soweth and he that reapeth may rejoice together.

And herein is that saying true, One soweth, and another reapeth.

I sent you to reap that whereon ye bestowed no labour: other men laboured, and ye are entered into their labours.

John 4:35-38

And he called (unto him) the twelve, and began to send them forth by two and two; and gave them power over unclean spirits;

And commanded them that they should take nothing for (their) journey, save a staff only; no scrip, no bread, no money in (their) purse:

But (be) shod with sandals; and not put on two coats.

And he said unto them, In what place soever ye enter into an house, there abide till ye depart from that place.

And whosoever shall not receive you, nor hear you, when ye depart thence, shake off the dust under your feet for a testimony against them. Verily I say unto you, It shall be more tolerable for Sodom and Gomorrha in the day of judgment, than for that city.

And they went out, and preached that men should repent.

Mark 6:7-12

For even when we were with you, this we commanded you, that if any would not work, neither
should he eat.

II Thessalonians 3:10

And whatsoever ye do, do (it) heartily, as to the
Lord, and not unto men;

Colossians 3:23

Let your speech (be) alway with grace, seasoned
with salt, that ye may know how ye ought to answer
every man.

Colossians 4:6

Wherefore seeing we also are compassed about
with so great a cloud of witnesses, let us lay aside
every weight, and the sin which doth so easily beset
(us), and let us run with patience the race that is set
before us,

Looking unto Jesus the author and finisher of
(our) faith; who for the joy that was set before him
endured the cross, despising the shame, and is set
down at the right hand of the throne of God.

Hebrews 12:1, 2

Service

For, brethren, ye have been called unto liberty; only (use) not liberty for an occasion to the flesh, but by love serve one another.

For all the law is fulfilled in one word, (even) in this; Thou shalt love thy neighbor as thyself.

Galatians 5:13, 14

Then said Jesus unto his disciples, If any (man) will come after me, let him deny himself, and take up his cross, and follow me.

For whosoever will save his life shall lose it: and whosoever will lose his life for my sake shall find it.

For what is a man profited, if he shall gain the whole world, and lose his own soul? or what shall a man give in exchange for his soul?

Matthew 16:24-26

Knowing that of the Lord ye shall receive the reward of the inheritance: for ye serve the Lord Christ.

Colossians 3:24

Servants, be obedient to them that are (your) masters according to the flesh, with fear and trembling, in singleness of your heart, as unto Christ;

Not with eyeservice, as menpleasers; but as the servants of Christ, doing the will of God from the heart;

With good will doing service, as to the Lord, and not to men:

Knowing that whatsoever good thing any man doeth, the same shall he receive of the Lord, whether (he be) bond or free.

Ephesians 6:5-8

If any man serve me, let him follow me; and where I am, there shall also my servant be: if any man serve me, him will (my) Father honour.

John 12:26

And, behold, a woman in the city, which was a sinner, when she knew that (Jesus) sat at meat in the Pharisee's house, brought an alabaster box of ointment,

And stood at his feet behind (him) weeping, and began to wash his feet with tears, and did wipe (them) with the hairs of her head, and kissed his feet, and anointed (them) with the ointment.

Luke 7:37, 38

Now it came to pass, as they went, that he entered into a certain village: and a certain woman named Martha received him into her house.

And she had a sister called Mary, which also sat at Jesus' feet, and heard his word.

But Martha was cumbered about much serving, and came to him, and said, Lord, dost thou not care that my sister hath left me to serve alone? bid her therefore that she help me.

And Jesus answered and said unto her, Martha, Martha, thou art careful and troubled about many things:

But one thing is needful: and Mary hath chosen that good part, which shall not be taken away from her.

Luke 10:38-42

No servant can serve two masters: for either he will hate the one, and love the other; or else he will hold to the one, and despise the other. Ye cannot serve God and mammon.

Luke 16:13

Charge them that are rich in this world, that they be not highminded, nor trust in uncertain riches, but in the living God, who giveth us richly all things to enjoy;

That they do good, that they be rich in good works, ready to distribute, willing to communicate;

Laying up in store for themselves a good foundation against the time to come, that they may lay hold on eternal life.

I Timothy 6:17-19

As every man hath received the gift, (even so) minister the same one to another, as good stewards of the manifold grace of God.

If any man speak, (let him speak) as the oracles of God; if any man minister, (let him do it) as of the ability which God giveth: that God in all things may be glorified through Jesus Christ, to whom be praise and dominion for ever and ever. Amen.

I Peter 4:10, 11

Ye have heard that it hath been said, An eye for an eye, and a tooth for a tooth:

But I say unto you, That ye resist not evil: but whosoever shall smite thee on thy right cheek, turn to him the other also.

And if any man will sue thee at the law, and take away thy coat, let him have (thy) cloke also.

And whosoever shall compel thee to go a mile, go with him twain.

Give to him that asketh thee, and from him that would borrow of thee turn not thou away.

Matthew 5:38-42

But it shall not be so among you: but whosoever will be great among you, let him be your minister;

And whosoever will be chief among you, let him be your servant:

Matthew 20:26, 27

And he sat down, and called the twelve, and saith unto them, If any man desire to be first, (the same) shall be last of all, and servant of all.

Mark 9:35

So after he had washed their feet, and had taken his garments, and was set down again, he said unto them, Know ye what I have done to you?

Ye call me Master and Lord: and ye say well; for (so) I am.

If I then, (your) Lord and Master, have washed your feet; ye also ought to wash one another's feet.

For I have given you an example, that ye should do as I have done to you.

John 13:12-15

I have coveted no man's silver, or gold, or apparel.

Yea, ye yourselves know, that these hands have ministered unto my necessities, and to them that were with me.

I have shewed you all things, how that so labouring ye ought to support the weak, and to remember the words of the Lord Jesus, how he said, It is more blessed to give than to receive.

Acts 20:33-35

(Let) nothing (be done) through strife or vainglory; but in lowliness of mind let each esteem other better than themselves.

Look not every man on his own things, but every man also on the things of others.

Let this mind be in you, which was also in Christ Jesus:

Who, being in the form of God, thought it not robbery to be equal with God:

But made himself of no reputation, and took upon him the form of a servant, and was made in the likeness of men:

And being found in fashion as a man, he humbled himself, and became obedient unto death, even the death of the cross.

Philippians 2:3-8

Investments

Lay not up for yourselves treasures upon earth, where moth and rust doth corrupt, and where thieves break through and steal:

But lay up for yourselves treasures in heaven, where neither moth nor rust doth corrupt, and where thieves do not break through nor steal:

For where your treasure is, there will your heart be also.

Matthew 6:19-21

He spake also this parable; A certain (man) had a fig tree planted in his vineyard; and he came and sought fruit thereon, and found none.

Then said he unto the dresser of his vineyard, Behold, these three years I come seeking fruit on this fig tree, and find none: cut it down; why cumbereth it the ground?

And he answering said unto him, Lord, let it alone this year also, till I shall dig about it, and dung (it):

And if it bear fruit, (well): and if not, (then) after that thou shalt cut it down.

Luke 13:6-9

Charge them that are rich in this world, that they be not highminded, nor trust in uncertain riches, but in the living God, who giveth us richly all things to enjoy;

That they do good, that they be rich in good works, ready to distribute, willing to communicate;

Laying up in store for themselves a good foundation against the time to come, that they may lay hold on eternal life.

I Timothy 6:17-19

And one of the company said unto him, Master, speak to my brother, that he divide the inheritance with me.

And he said unto him, Man, who made me a judge or a divider over you?

And he said unto them, Take heed, and beware of covetousness: for a man's life consisteth not in the abundance of the things which he possesseth.

And he spake a parable unto them, saying, The ground of a certain rich man brought forth plentifully:

And he thought within himself, saying, What shall I do, because I have no room where to bestow my fruits?

And he said, This will I do: I will pull down my barns, and build greater; and there will I bestow all my fruits and my goods.

And I will say to my soul, Soul, thou hast much goods laid up for many years; take thine ease, eat, drink, (and) be merry.

But God said unto him, (Thou) fool, this night thy soul shall be required of thee: then whose shall those things be, which thou hast provided?

So (is) he that layeth up treasure for himself, and is not rich toward God.

Luke 12:13-21

His lord answered and said unto him, (Thou) wicked and slothful servant, thou knewest that I reap where I sowed not, and gather where I have not strawed:

Thou oughtest therefore to have put my money to the exchangers, and (then) at my coming I should have received mine own with usury.

Matthew 25:26, 27

Now when Jesus heard these things, he said unto him, Yet lackest thou one thing: sell all that thou hast, and distribute unto the poor, and thou shalt have treasure in heaven: and come, follow me.

Luke 18:22

And it came to pass, that when he was returned, having received the kingdom, then he commanded these servants to be called unto him, to whom he had given the money, that he might know how much every man had gained by trading.

Then came the first, saying, Lord, thy pound hath gained ten pounds.

And he said unto him, Well, thou good servant: because thou hast been faithful in a very little, have thou authority over ten cities.

And the second came, saying, Lord, thy pound hath gained five pounds.

And he said likewise to him, Be thou also over five cities.

And another came, saying, Lord, behold, (here is) thy pound, which I have kept laid up in a napkin:

For I feared thee, because thou art an austere man: thou takest up that thou layedst not down, and reapest that thou didst not sow.

And he saith unto him, Out of thine own mouth will I judge thee, (thou) wicked servant. Thou knewest that I was an austere man, taking up that I laid not down, and reaping that I did not sow:

Wherefore then gavest not thou my money into the bank, that at my coming I might have required mine own with usury?

And he said unto them that stood by, Take from him the pound, and give (it) to him that hath ten pounds.

(And they said unto him, Lord, he hath ten pounds.)

For I say unto you, That unto every one which hath shall be given; and from him that hath not, even that he hath shall be taken away from him.

Luke 19:15-26

And he looked up, and saw the rich men casting their gifts into the treasury.

And he saw also a certain poor widow casting in thither two mites.

And he said, Of a truth I say unto you, that this poor widow hath cast in more than they all:

For all these have of their abundance cast in unto the offerings of God: but she of her penury hath cast in all the living that she had.

Luke 21:1-4

My son, if thou be surety for thy friend, (if) thou hast stricken thy hand with a stranger,

Thou art snared with the words of thy mouth,
thou art taken with the words of thy mouth.

Proverbs 6:1, 2

In the house of the righteous (is) much
treasure: but in the revenues of the wicked is trouble.

Proverbs 15:6

Better (is) a little with righteousness than
great revenues without right.

Proverbs 16:8

When thou vowest a vow unto God, defer not
to pay it; for (he hath) no pleasure in fools: pay that
which thou hast vowed.
Better (is it) that thou shouldest not vow, than
that thou shouldest vow and not pay.

Ecclesiastes 5:4, 5

Go to the ant, thou sluggard; consider her
ways, and be wise:
Which having no guide, overseer, or ruler,
Provideth her meat in the summer, (and)
gathereth her food in the harvest.

Proverbs 6:6-8

Adaptability To Change

Not that I speak in respect of want: for I have learned, in whatsoever state I am, (therewith) to be content.

I know both how to be abased, and I know how to abound: every where and in all things I am instructed both to be full and to be hungry, both to abound and to suffer need.

Philippians 4:11, 12

To every (thing there is) a season, and a time to every purpose under the heaven:

A time to be born, and a time to die; a time to plant, and a time to pluck up (that which is) planted;

A time to kill, and a time to heal; a time to break down, and a time to build up;

A time to weep, and a time to laugh; a time to mourn, and a time to dance;

A time to cast away stones, and a time to gather stones together; a time to embrace, and a time to refrain from embracing;

A time to get, and a time to lose; a time to keep, and a time to cast away;

A time to rend, and a time to sew; a time to keep silence, and a time to speak;

A time to love, and a time to hate; a time of war, and a time of peace.

Ecclesiastes 3:1-8

Unto the upright there ariseth light in the darkness: (he is) gracious, and full of compassion, and righteous.

A good man sheweth favour, and lendeth: he will guide his affairs with discretion.

Psalms 112:4, 5

Without counsel purposes are disappointed: but in the multitude of counsellors they are established.

A man hath joy by the answer of his mouth: and a word (spoken) in due season, how good (is it)!

Proverbs 15:22, 23

Commit thy works unto the LORD, and thy thoughts shall be established.

Proverbs 16:3

I beseech you therefore, brethren, by the mercies of God, that ye present your bodies a living sacrifice, holy, acceptable unto God, (which is) your reasonable service.

And be not conformed to this world: but be ye transformed by the renewing of your mind, that ye may prove what (is) that good, and acceptable, and perfect, will of God.

Romans 12:1, 2

I can do all things through Christ which strengtheneth me.

Philippians 4:13

If any of you lack wisdom, let him ask of God, that giveth to all (men) liberally, and upbraideth not; and it shall be given him.

But let him ask in faith, nothing wavering. For he that wavereth is like a wave of the sea driven with the wind and tossed.

A double minded man (is) unstable in all his ways.

James 1:5, 6, 8

Every prudent (man) dealeth with knowledge: but a fool layeth open (his) folly.

Proverbs 13:16

Who (is) wise, and he shall understand these (things)? prudent, and he shall know them? for the ways of the LORD (are) right, and the just shall walk in them: but the transgressors shall fall therein.

Hosea 14:9

And take heed to yourselves, lest at any time your hearts be overcharged with surfeiting, and drunkenness, and cares of this life, and (so) that day come upon you unawares.

For as a snare shall it come on all them that dwell on the face of the whole earth.

Watch ye therefore, and pray always, that ye may be accounted worthy to escape all these things that shall come to pass, and to stand before the Son of man. *Luke 21:34-36*

Biblical Ethics For Your Business...

Loyalty

He that is faithful in that which is least is faithful also in much: and he that is unjust in the least is unjust also in much.

If therefore ye have not been faithful in the unrighteous mammon, who will commit to your trust the true (riches)?

And if ye have not been faithful in that which is another man's, who shall give you that which is your own?

No servant can serve two masters: for either he will hate the one, and love the other; or else he will hold to the one, and despise the other. Ye cannot serve God and mammon.

Luke 16:10-13

And he arose, and came to his father. But when he was yet a great way off, his father saw him, and had compassion, and ran, and fell on his neck, and kissed him.

And the son said to him, Father, I have sinned against heaven, and in thy sight, and am no more worthy to be called thy son.

But the father said to his servants, Bring forth the best robe, and put (it) on him; and put a ring on his hand, and shoes on (his) feet:

And bring hither the fatted calf, and kill (it); and let us eat, and be merry:

For this my son was dead, and is alive again; he was lost, and is found. And they began to be merry.

Luke 15:20-24

If my people, which are called by my name, shall humble themselves, and pray, and seek my face, and turn from their wicked ways; then will I hear from heaven, and will forgive their sin, and will heal their land.

II Chronicles 7:14

His lord said unto him, Well done, thou good and faithful servant: thou hast been faithful over a few things, I will make thee ruler over many things: enter thou into the joy of thy Lord.

Matthew 25:21

Let a man so account of us, as of the ministers of Christ, and stewards of the mysteries of God.

Moreover it is required in stewards, that a man be found faithful.

I Corinthians 4:1, 2

And the Lord said, Simon, Simon, behold, Satan hath desired (to have) you, that he may sift (you) as wheat:

But I have prayed for thee, that thy faith fail not: and when thou art converted, strengthen thy brethren.

And he said unto him, Lord, I am ready to go with thee, both into prison, and to death.

And he said, I tell thee, Peter, the cock shall not crow this day, before that thou shalt thrice deny that thou knowest me.

Luke 22:31-34

We then that are strong ought to bear the infirmities of the weak, and not to please ourselves.

Let every one of us please (his) neighbour for (his) good to edification.

Romans 15:1, 2

Then said Jesus unto his disciples, If any (man) will come after me, let him deny himself, and take up his cross, and follow me.

Matthew 16:24

And he came out, and went, as he was wont, to the mount of Olives; and his disciples also followed him.

And when he was at the place, he said unto them, Pray that ye enter not into temptation.

And he was withdrawn from them about a stone's cast, and kneeled down, and prayed,

Saying, Father, if thou be willing, remove this cup from me: nevertheless not my will, but thine, be done.

Luke 22:39-42

From that (time) many of his disciples went back, and walked no more with him.

Then said Jesus unto the twelve, Will ye also go away?

Then Simon Peter answered him, Lord, to whom shall we go? thou hast the words of eternal life.

And we believe and are sure that thou art that Christ, the Son of the living God.

John 6:66-69

Thou therefore endure hardness, as a good soldier of Jesus Christ.

II Timothy 2:3

Therefore, brethren, stand fast, and hold the traditions which ye have been taught, whether by word, or our epistle.

II Thessalonians 2:15

But ye, brethren, be not weary in well doing.

II Thessalonians 3:13

Therefore, my brethren dearly beloved and longed for, my joy and crown, so stand fast in the Lord, (my) dearly beloved.

Philippians 4:1

And let us not be weary in well doing: for in due season we shall reap, if we faint not.

Galatians 6:9

Therefore, my beloved brethren, be ye stedfast, unmoveable, always abounding in the work of the Lord, forasmuch as ye know that your labour is not in vain in the Lord.

I Corinthians 15:58

Watch ye, stand fast in the faith, quit you like men, be strong.

I Corinthians 16:13

Accountability

So then every one of us shall give account of himself to God.

Romans 14:12

But he that knew not, and did commit things worthy of stripes, shall be beaten with few (stripes). For unto whomsoever much is given, of him shall be much required: and to whom men have committed much, of him they will ask the more.

Luke 12:48

Wherefore let him that thinketh he standeth take heed lest he fall.

There hath no temptation taken you but such as is common to man: but God (is) faithful, who will not suffer you to be tempted above that ye are able; but will with the temptation also make a way to escape, that ye may be able to bear (it)

I Corinthians 10:12, 13

Moreover it is required in stewards, that a man be found faithful.

I Corinthians 4:2

The Pharisee stood and prayed thus with himself, God, I thank thee, that I am not as other men (are), extortioners, unjust, adulterers, or even as this publican.

And the publican, standing afar off, would not lift up so much as (his) eyes unto heaven, but smote upon his breast, saying, God be merciful to me a sinner.

I tell you, this man went down to his house justified (rather) than the other: for every one that exalteth himself shall be abased; and he that humbleth himself shall be exalted.

Luke 18:11, 13, 14

Obey them that have the rule over you, and submit yourselves: for they watch for your souls, as they that must give account, that they may do it with joy, and not with grief: for that (is) unprofitable for you.

Hebrews 13:17

Stand fast therefore in the liberty wherewith Christ hath made us free, and be not entangled again with the yoke of bondage.

Galatians 5:1

And he said unto his disciples, There was a certain rich man, which had a steward; and the same was accused unto him that he had wasted his goods.

And he called him, and said unto him, How is it that I hear this of thee? give an account of thy stewardship; for thou mayest be no longer steward.

Luke 16:1, 2

Watch ye therefore, and pray always, that ye may be accounted worthy to escape all these things that shall come to pass, and to stand before the Son of man.

Luke 21:36

He spake also this parable; A certain (man) had a fig tree planted in his vineyard; and he came and sought fruit thereon, and found none.

Then said he unto the dresser of his vineyard, Behold, these three years I come seeking fruit on this fig tree, and find none: cut it down; why cumbereth it the ground?

And he answering said unto him, Lord, let it alone this year also, till I shall dig about it, and dung (it):

And if it bear fruit, (well): and if not, (then) after that thou shalt cut it down.

Luke 13:6-9

As every man hath received the gift, (even so) minister the same one to another, as good stewards of the manifold grace of God.

I Peter 4:10

If thou be wise, thou shalt be wise for thyself: but (if) thou scornest, thou alone shalt bear (it).

Proverbs 9:12

Therefore is the kingdom of heaven likened unto a certain king, which would take account of his servants.

Matthew 18:23

But I say unto you, That every idle word that men shall speak, they shall give account thereof in the day of judgment.

Matthew 12:36

He said therefore, A certain nobleman went into a far country to receive for himself a kingdom, and to return.

And he called his ten servants, and delivered them ten pounds, and said unto them, Occupy till I come.

But his citizens hated him, and sent a message after him, saying, We will not have this (man) to reign over us.

And it came to pass, that when he was returned, having received the kingdom, then he commanded these servants to be called unto him, to whom he had given the money, that he might know how much every man had gained by trading.

Luke 19:12-15

But God said unto him, (Thou) fool, this night thy soul shall be required of thee: then whose shall those things be, which thou hast provided?

Luke 12:20

The fathers shall not be put to death for the children, neither shall the children be put to death for the fathers: every man shall be put to death for his own sin.

Deuteronomy 24:16

And be it indeed (that) I have erred, mine error remaineth with myself.

Job 19:4

Who art thou that judgest another man's servant? to his own master he standeth or falleth. Yea, he shall be holden up: for God is able to make him stand.

Romans 14:4

We then that are strong ought to bear the infirmities of the weak, and not to please ourselves.

Let every one of us please (his) neighbor for (his) good to edification.

Romans 15:1, 2

Brethren, if a man be overtaken in a fault, ye which are spiritual, restore such an one in the spirit of meekness; considering thyself, lest thou also be tempted.

Galatians 6:1

But every one shall die for his own iniquity: every man that eateth the sour grape, his teeth shall be set on edge.

Jeremiah 31:30

The soul that sinneth, it shall die. The son shall not bear the iniquity of the father, neither shall the father bear the iniquity of the son: the righteousness of the righteous shall be upon him, and the wickedness of the wicked shall be upon him.

Ezekiel 18:20

O Timothy, keep that which is committed to thy trust, avoiding profane (and) vain babblings, and oppositions of science falsely so called:

Which some professing have erred concerning the faith. Grace (be) with thee. Amen.

I Timothy 6:20, 21

Competition

The discretion of a man deferreth his anger; and (it is) his glory to pass over a transgression.
Proverbs 19:11

Wherefore, my beloved brethren, let every man be swift to hear, slow to speak, slow to wrath:
James 1:19

Therefore all things whatsoever ye would that men should do to you, do ye even so to them: for this is the law and the prophets.
Matthew 7:12

Put on the whole armour of God, that ye may be able to stand against the wiles of the devil.

For we wrestle not against flesh and blood, but against principalities, against powers, against the rulers of the darkness of this world, against spiritual wickedness in high (places).

Wherefore take unto you the whole armour of God, that ye may be able to withstand in the evil day, and having done all, to stand.

Stand therefore, having your loins girt about with truth, and having on the breastplate of righteousness;

And your feet shod with the preparation of the gospel of peace;

Above all, taking the shield of faith, wherewith ye shall be able to quench all the fiery darts of the wicked.

And take the helmet of salvation, and the sword of the Spirit, which is the word of God:

Ephesians 6:11-17

Pride (goeth) before destruction, and an haughty spirit before a fall.

Better (it is to be) of an humble spirit with the lowly, than to divide the spoil with the proud.

Proverbs 16:18, 19

He that handleth a matter wisely shall find good: and whoso trusteth in the LORD, happy (is) he.

Proverbs 16:20

For though we walk in the flesh, we do not war after the flesh:

(For the weapons of our warfare (are) not carnal, but mighty through God to the pulling down of strong holds;)

II Corinthians 10:3, 4

(Let your) conversation (be) without covetousness; (and be) content with such things as ye have: for he hath said, I will never leave thee, nor forsake thee.

So that we may boldly say, The Lord (is) my helper, and I will not fear what man shall do unto me.

Hebrews 13:5, 6

And he said unto them, Take heed, and beware of covetousness: for a man's life consisteth not in the abundance of the things which he possesseth.

Luke 12:15

Better (is) the end of a thing than the beginning thereof: (and) the patient in spirit (is) better than the proud in spirit.

Be not hasty in thy spirit to be angry: for anger resteth in the bosom of fools.

Ecclesiastes 7:8, 9

And let us not be weary in well doing: for in due season we shall reap, if we faint not.

Galatians 6:9

But avoid foolish questions, and genealogies, and contentions, and strivings about the law; for they are unprofitable and vain.

Titus 3:9

He that is greedy of gain troubleth his own house; but he that hateth gifts shall live.

Proverbs 15:27

And that ye study to be quiet, and to do your own business, and to work with your own hands, as we commanded you;

That ye may walk honestly toward them that are without, and (that) ye may have lack of nothing.

I Thessalonians 4:11, 12

He that is of a proud heart stirreth up strife: but he that putteth his trust in the LORD shall be made fat.

He that trusteth in his own heart is a fool: but whoso walketh wisely, he shall be delivered.

Proverbs 28:25, 26

And the servant of the Lord must not strive;
but be gentle unto all (men), apt to teach, patient,
In meekness instructing those that oppose
themselves; if God peradventure will give them
repentance to the acknowledging of the truth;

II Timothy 2:24, 25

Strive not with a man without cause, if he
have done thee no harm.

Proverbs 3:30

No weapon that is formed against thee shall
prosper; and every tongue (that) shall rise against
thee in judgment thou shalt condemn. This (is) the
heritage of the servants of the LORD, and their
righteousness (is) of me, saith the LORD.

Isaiah 54:17

Good Name & Reputation

A (good) name (is) rather to be chosen than great riches, (and) loving favour rather than silver and gold.

Proverbs 22:1

A good name (is) better than precious ointment; and the day of death than the day of one's birth.

Ecclesiastes 7:1

Dead flies cause the ointment of the apothecary to send forth a stinkng savour: (so doth) a little folly him that is in reputation for wisdom (and) honour.

Ecclesiastes 10:1

Then Peter and the (other) apostles answered and said, We ought to obey God rather than men.

Him hath God exalted with his right hand (to be) a Prince and a Saviour, for to give repentance to Israel, and forgiveness of sins.

And we are his witnesses of these things; and (so is) also the Holy Ghost, whom God hath given to them that obey him.

When they heard (that), they were cut (to the heart), and took counsel to slay them.

Then stood there up one in the council, a Pharisee, named Gamaliel, a doctor of the law, had in reputation among all the people, and commanded to put the apostles forth a little space;

And said unto them, Ye men of Israel, take heed to yourselves what ye intend to do as touching these men.

Acts 5:29, 31-35

Let this mind be in you, which was also in Christ Jesus:

Who, being in the form of God, thought it not robbery to be equal with God:

But made himself of no reputation, and took upon him the form of a servant, and was made in the likeness of men:

And being found in fashion as a man, he humbled himself, and became obedient unto death, even the death of the cross.

Wherefore God also hath highly exalted him, and given him a name which is above every name:

That at the name of Jesus every knee should bow, of (things) in heaven, and (things) in earth, and (things) under the earth;

And (that) every tongue should confess that Jesus Christ (is) Lord, to the glory of God the Father.
Philippians 2:5-11

And in those days, when the number of the disciples was multiplied, there arose a murmuring of the Grecians against the Hebrews, because their widows were neglected in the daily ministration.

Then the twelve called the multitude of the disciples (unto them), and said, It is not reason that we should leave the word of God, and serve tables.

Wherefore, brethren, look ye out among you seven men of honest report, full of the Holy Ghost and wisdom, whom we may appoint over this business.

But we will give ourselves continually to prayer, and to the ministry of the word.

And the saying pleased the whole multitude: and they chose Stephen, a man full of faith and of the Holy Ghost, and Philip, and Prochorus, and Nicanor, and Timon, and Parmenas, and Nicolas a proselyte of Antioch:

Whom they set before the apostles: and when they had prayed, they laid (their) hands on them.

Acts 6:1-6

Then Peter went down to the men which were sent unto him from Cornelius; and said, Behold, I am he whom ye seek: what (is) the cause wherefore ye are come?

And they said, Cornelius the centurion, a just man, and one that feareth God, and of good report among all the nation of the Jews, was warned from God by an holy angel to send for thee into his house, and to hear words of thee.

Acts 10:21, 22

Let your light so shine before men, that they may see your good works, and glorify your Father which is in heaven.

Matthew 5:16

A good man out of the good treasure of his heart bringeth forth that which is good; and an evil man out of the evil treasure of his heart bringeth forth that which is evil: for of the abundance of the heart his mouth speaketh.

Luke 6:45

A good (man) obtaineth favour of the LORD: but a man of wicked devices will he condemn.

Proverbs 12:2

A good man sheweth favour, and lendeth: he will guide his affairs with discretion.

Psalms 112:5

The steps of a (good) man are ordered by the LORD: and he delighteth in his way.

Though he fall, he shall not be utterly cast down: for the LORD upholdeth (him with) his hand.

Psalms 37:23, 24

Blessed (is) the man that walketh not in the counsel of the ungodly, nor standeth in the way of sinners, nor sitteth in the seat of the scornful.

But his delight (is) in the law of the LORD; and in his law doth he meditate day and night.

Psalms 1:1, 2

He that hath knowledge spareth his words: (and) a man of understanding is of an excellent spirit.

Proverbs 17:27

Ye are the salt of the earth: but if the salt have lost his savour, wherewith shall it be salted? it is thenceforth good for nothing, but to be cast out, and to be trodden under foot of men.

Ye are the light of the world. A city that is set on an hill cannot be hid.

Neither do men light a candle, and put it under a bushel, but on a candlestick; and it giveth light unto all that are in the house.

Let your light so shine before men, that they may see your good works, and glorify your Father which is in heaven.

Matthew 5:13-16

Courage & Convictions

Therefore, my beloved brethren, be ye steadfast, unmoveable, always abounding in the work of the Lord, forasmuch as ye know that your labour is not in vain in the Lord.

I Corinthians 15:58

Blessed (is) the man that endureth temptation: for when he is tried, he shall receive the crown of life, which the Lord hath promised to them that love him.

James 1:12

Only let your conversation be as it becometh the gospel of Christ: that whether I come and see you, or else be absent, I may hear of your affairs, that ye stand fast in one spirit, with one mind striving together for the faith of the gospel.

Philippians 1:27

Stand fast therefore in the liberty wherewith Christ hath made us free, and be not entangled again with the yoke of bondage.

Galatians 5:1

Ye therefore, beloved, seeing ye know (these things) before, beware lest ye also, being led away with the error of the wicked, fall from your own steadfastness.

II Peter 3:17

Be sober, be vigilant; because your adversary the devil, as a roaring lion, walketh about, seeking whom he may devour:

Whom resist stedfast in the faith, knowing that the same afflictions are accomplished in your brethren that are in the world.

But the God of all grace, who hath called us unto his eternal glory by Christ Jesus, after that ye have suffered a while, make you perfect, stablish, strengthen, settle (you).

I Peter 5:8-10

Be strong and of a good courage, fear not, nor be afraid of them: for the LORD thy God, he (it is) that doth go with thee; he will not fail thee, nor forsake thee.

Deuteronomy 31:6

Be strong and of a good courage: for unto this people shalt thou divide for an inheritance the land, which I sware unto their fathers to give them.

Only be thou strong and very courageous, that thou mayest observe to do according to all the law, which Moses my servant commanded thee: turn not from it (to) the right hand or (to) the left, that thou mayest prosper whithersoever thou goest.

This book of the law shall not depart out of thy mouth; but thou shalt meditate therein day and night, that thou mayest observe to do according to all that is written therein: for then thou shalt make thy way prosperous, and then thou shalt have good success.

Have not I commanded thee? Be strong and of a good courage; be not afraid, neither be thou dismayed: for the LORD thy God (is) with thee whithersoever thou goest.

Joshua 1:6-9

Be strong and courageous, be not afraid nor dismayed for the king of Assyria, nor for all the multitude that (is) with him: for (there be) more with us than with him:

II Chronicles 32:7

And David unto said to Saul, Let no man's heart fail because of him; thy servant will go and fight with this Philistine.

And Saul said to David, Thou art not able to go against this Philistine to fight with him: for thou (art but) a youth, and he a man of war from his youth.

And Saul armed David with his armour, and he put an helmet of brass upon his head; also he armed him with a coat of mail.

And David girded his sword upon his armour, and he assayed to go; for he had not proved (it). And David said unto Saul, I cannot go with these; for I have not proved (them). And David put them off him.

And he took his staff in his hand, and chose him five smooth stones out of the brook, and put them in a shepherd's bag which he had, even in a scrip; and his sling (was) in his hand: and he drew near to the Philistine.

Then said David to the Philistine, Thou comest to me with a sword, and with a spear, and with a shield: but I come to thee in the name of the LORD of hosts, the God of the armies of Israel, whom thou hast defied.

And all this assembly shall know that the LORD saveth not with sword and spear: for the battle (is) the LORD'S, and he will give you into our hands.

And it came to pass, when the Philistine arose, and came and drew nigh to meet David, that David hasted, and ran toward the army to meet the Philistine.

And David put his hand in his bag, and took thence a stone, and slang (it), and smote the Philistine in his forehead, that the stone sunk into his forehead; and he fell upon his face to the earth.

I Samuel 17:32, 33, 38-40, 45, 47-49

Then Nebuchadnezzar in (his) rage and fury commanded to bring Shadrach, Meshach, and Abed-nego. Then they brought these men before the king.

Nebuchadnezzar spake and said unto them, (Is it) true, O Shadrach, Meshach, and Abed-nego, do not ye serve my gods, nor worship the golden image which I have set up?

Now if ye be ready that at what time ye hear the sound of the cornet, flute, harp, sackbut, psaltery, and dulcimer, and all kinds of music, ye fall down and worship the image which I have made; (well): but if ye worship not, ye shall be cast the same hour into the midst of a burning fiery furnace; and who (is) that God that shall deliver you out of my hands?

Shadrach, Meshach, and Abed- nego, answered and said to the king, O Nebuchadnezzar, we (are) not careful to answer thee in this matter.

If it be (so), our God whom we serve is able to deliver us from the burning fiery furnace, and he will deliver (us) out of thine hand, O king.

But if not, be it known unto thee, O king, that we will not serve thy gods, nor worship the golden image which thou hast set up.

And these three men, Shadrach, Meshach, and Abed-nego, fell down bound into the midst of the burning fiery furnace.

Then Nebuchadnezzar the king was astonied, and rose up in haste, (and) spake, and said unto his counsellors, Did not we cast three men bound into the midst of the fire? They answered and said unto the king, True, O king.

He answered and said, Lo, I see four men loose, walking in the midst of the fire, and they have no hurt; and the form of the fourth is like the Son of God.

Daniel 3:13-18, 23-25

Therefore will not we fear, though the earth be removed, and though the mountains be carried into the midst of the sea;

Psalms 46:2

His heart (is) established, he shall not be afraid, until he see (his desire) upon his enemies.

Psalms 112:8

Behold, God (is) my salvation; I will trust, and not be afraid: for the LORD JEHOVAH (is) my strength and (my) song; he also is become my salvation.

Isaiah 12:2

Then saith Pilate unto him, Speakest thou not unto me? knowest thou not that I have power to crucify thee, and have power to release thee?

Jesus answered, Thou couldest have no power (at all) against me, except it were given thee from above: therefore he that delivered me unto thee hath the greater sin.

John 19:10, 11

Fight the good fight of faith, lay hold on eternal life, whereunto thou art also called, and hast professed a good profession before many witnesses.

I Timothy 6:12

To him that overcometh will I grant to sit with me in my throne, even as I also overcame, and am set down with my Father in his throne.

Revelation 3:21

For the eyes of the LORD run to and fro throughout the whole earth, to shew himself strong in the behalf of (them) whose heart (is) perfect toward him. Herein thou hast done foolishly: therefore from henceforth thou shalt have wars.

II Chronicles 16:9

He shall cover thee with his feathers, and under his wings shalt thou trust: his truth (shall be thy) shield and buckler.

Psalms 91:4

Ye stiffnecked and uncircumcised in heart and ears, ye do always resist the Holy Ghost: as your fathers (did), so (do) ye.

When they heard these things, they were cut to the heart, and they gnashed on him with (their) teeth.

Then they cried out with a loud voice, and stopped their ears, and ran upon him with one accord,

And cast (him) out of the city, and stoned (him): and the witnesses laid down their clothes at a young man's feet, whose name was Saul.

And they stoned Stephen, calling upon (God), and saying, Lord Jesus, receive my spirit.

And he kneeled down, and cried with a loud voice, Lord, lay not this sin to their charge. And when he had said this, he fell asleep.

Acts 7:51, 54, 57-60

And Jesus went into the temple of God, and cast out all them that sold and bought in the temple, and overthrew the tables of the moneychangers, and the seats of them that sold doves,

And said unto them, It is written, My house shall be called the house of prayer; but ye have made it a den of thieves.

Matthew 21:12, 13

I beseech you therefore, brethren, by the mercies of God, that ye present your bodies a living sacrifice, holy, acceptable unto God, (which is) your reasonable service.

And be not conformed to this world: but be ye transformed by the renewing of your mind, that ye may prove what (is) that good, and acceptable, and perfect, will of God.

Romans 12:1, 2

For the Lord GOD will help me; therefore shall I not be confounded: therefore have I set my face like a flint, and I know that I shall not be ashamed.

Isaiah 50:7

For I am not ashamed of the gospel of Christ: for it is the power of God unto salvation to every one that believeth; to the Jew first, and also to the Greek.

Romans 1:16

Watch ye, stand fast in the faith, quit you like men, be strong.

I Corinthians 16:13

Wherefore take unto you the whole armour of God, that ye may be able to withstand in the evil day, and having done all, to stand.

Ephesians 6:13

Work Ethic

Whatsoever thy hand findeth to do, do it with thy might; for there is no work, nor device, nor knowledge, nor wisdom, in the grave, whither thou goest.

Ecclesiastes 9:10

And whatsoever ye do, do it heartily, as unto the Lord, and not unto men.

Colossians 3:23

Trust in the LORD, and do good; (so) shalt thou dwell in the land, and verily thou shalt be fed.

Psalms 37:3

And let the beauty of the LORD our God be upon us: and establish thou the work of our hands upon us; yea, the work of our hands establish thou it.

Psalms 90:17

Take heed that ye do not your alms before men, to be seen of them: otherwise ye have no reward of your Father which is in heaven.

Therefore when thou doest (thine) alms, do not sound a trumpet before thee, as the hypocrites do in the synagogues and in the streets, that they may have glory of men. Verily I say unto you, They have their reward.

But when thou doest alms, let not thy left hand know what thy right hand doeth:

That thine alms may be in secret: and thy Father which seeth in secret himself shall reward thee openly.

Matthew 6:1-4

For we are his workmanship, created in Christ Jesus unto good works, which God hath before ordained that we should walk in them.

Ephesians 2:10

I have planted, Apollos watered; but God gave the increase.

So then neither is he that planteth any thing, neither he that watereth; but God that giveth the increase.

Now he that planteth and he that watereth are one: and every man shall receive his own reward according to his own labour.

I Corinthians 3:6-8

And God (is) able to make all grace abound toward you; that ye, always having all sufficiency in all (things), may abound to every good work:

II Corinthians 9:8

But let every man prove his own work, and then shall he have rejoicing in himself alone, and not in another.

Galatians 6:4

For it is God which worketh in you both to will and to do of (his) good pleasure.

Philippians 2:13

Charge them that are rich in this world, that they be not highminded, nor trust in uncertain riches, but in the living God, who giveth us richly all things to enjoy;

That they do good, that they be rich in good works, ready to distribute, willing to communicate;

Laying up in store for themselves a good foundation against the time to come, that they may lay hold on eternal life.

I Timothy 6:17-19

(This is) a faithful saying, and these things I will that thou affirm constantly, that they which have believed in God might be careful to maintain good works. These things are good and profitable unto men.

Titus 3:8

And let ours also learn to maintain good works for necessary uses, that they be not unfruitful.

Titus 3:14

For God (is) not unrighteous to forget your work and labour of love, which ye have shewed toward his name, in that ye have ministered to the saints, and do minister.

Hebrews 6:10

And let us consider one another to provoke unto love and to good works:

Hebrews 10:24

Who (is) a wise man and endued with knowledge among you? let him shew out of a good conversation his works with meekness of wisdom.

James 3:13

And I heard a voice from heaven saying unto me, Write, Blessed (are) the dead which die in the Lord from henceforth: Yea, saith the Spirit, that they may rest from their labours; and their works do follow them.

Revelation 14:13

Blessed (are) they that do his commandments, that they may have right to the tree of life, and may enter in through the gates into the city.

Revelation 22:14

Biblical Standards With Business Associates...

Business Relationships

Therefore all things whatsoever ye would that men should do to you, do ye even so to them: for this is the law and the prophets.

Matthew 7:12

Ye have heard that it hath been said, Thou shalt love thy neighbour, and hate thine enemy.

But I say unto you, Love your enemies, bless them that curse you, do good to them that hate you, and pray for them which despitefully use you, and persecute you;

That ye may be the children of your Father which is in heaven: for he maketh his sun to rise on the evil and on the good, and sendeth rain on the just and on the unjust.

For if ye love them which love you, what reward have ye? do not even the publicans the same?

And if ye salute your brethren only, what do ye more than others? do not even the publicans so?

Be ye therefore perfect, even as your Father which is in heaven is perfect.

Matthew 5:43-48

If there be among you a poor man of one of thy brethren within any of thy gates in thy land which the LORD thy God giveth thee, thou shalt not harden thine heart, nor shut thine hand from thy poor brother:

But thou shalt open thine hand wide unto him, and shalt surely lend him sufficient for his need, (in that) which he wanteth.

Deuteronomy 15:7, 8

Have we not all one father? hath not one God created us? why do we deal treacherously every man against his brother, by profaning the covenant of our fathers?

Malachi 2:10

(A Song of degrees of David.) Behold, how good and how pleasant (it is) for brethren to dwell together in unity!

Psalms 133:1

Whoso causeth the righteous to go astray in an evil way, he shall fall himself into his own pit: but the upright shall have good (things) in possession.

Proverbs 28:10

Thou shalt not defraud thy neighbour, neither rob (him): the wages of him that is hired shall not abide with thee all night until the morning.

Leviticus 19:13

Thou shalt not avenge, nor bear any grudge against the children of thy people, but thou shalt love thy neighbour as thyself: I (am) the LORD.

Leviticus 19:18

Ye shall do no unrighteousness in judgment, in meteyard, in weight, or in measure.

Just balances, just weights, a just ephah, and a just hin, shall ye have: I (am) the LORD your God, which brought you out of the land of Egypt.

Leviticus 19:35, 36

And if thou sell ought unto thy neighbour, or buyest (ought) of thy neighbour's hand, ye shall not oppress one another:

Leviticus 25:14

An high look, and a proud heart, (and) the plowing of the wicked, (is) sin.

Proverbs 21:4

Say not, I will do so to him as he hath done to me: I will render to the man according to his work.

Proverbs 24:29

A man (that hath) friends must shew himself friendly: and there is a friend (that) stricketh closer than a brother.

Proverbs 18:24

A friend loveth at all times, and a brother is born for adversity.

A man void of understanding striketh hands, (and) becometh surety in the presence of his friend.

Proverbs 17:17, 18

Thine own friend, and thy father's friend, forsake not; neither go into thy brother's house in the day of thy calamity: (for) better (is) a neighbour (that is) near than a brother far off.

Proverbs 27:10

Iron sharpeneth iron; so a man sharpeneth the countenance of his friend.

Proverbs 27:17

Two (are) better than one; because they have a good reward for their labour.
For if they fall, the one will lift up his fellow: but woe to him (that is) alone when he falleth; for (he hath) not another to help him up.

Ecclesiastes 4:9, 10

Greater love hath no man than this, that a man lay down his life for his friends.
Ye are my friends, if ye do whatsoever I command you.

John 15:13, 14

And Abram said unto Lot, Let there be no strife, I pray thee, between me and thee, and between my herdmen and thy herdmen; for we (be) brethren.

Genesis 13:8

But I say unto you, That whosoever is angry with his brother without a cause shall be in danger of the judgment: and whosoever shall say to his brother, Raca, shall be in danger of the council: but whosoever shall say, Thou fool, shall be in danger of hell fire.

Matthew 5:22

A new commandment I give unto you, That ye love one another; as I have loved you, that ye also love one another.

John 13:34

Brethren, if a man be overtaken in a fault, ye which are spiritual, restore such an one in the spirit of meekness; considering thyself, lest thou also be tempted.

Galatians 6:1

And if any man obey not our word by this epistle, note that man, and have no company with him, that he may be ashamed.

Yet count (him) not as an enemy, but admonish (him) as a brother.

II Thessalonians 3:14, 15

He that saith he is in the light, and hateth his brother, is in darkness even until now.

I John 2:9

Hereby perceive we the love of God, because he laid down his life for us: and we ought to lay down our lives for the brethren.

But whoso hath this world's good, and seeth his brother have need, and shutteth up his bowels (of compassion) from him, how dwelleth the love of God in him?

My little children, let us not love in word, neither in tongue; but in deed and in truth.

I John 3:16-18

Honesty

Wherefore putting away lying, speak every man truth with his neighbour: for we are members one of another.

Ephesians 4:25

Therefore seeing we have this ministry, as we have received mercy, we faint not;

But have renounced the hidden things of dishonesty, not walking in craftiness, nor handling the word of God deceitfully; but by manifestation of the truth commending ourselves to every man's conscience in the sight of God.

II Corinthians 4:1, 2

And that ye study to be quiet, and to do your own business, and to work with your own hands, as we commended you;

That ye may walk honestly toward them that are without, and (that) ye may have lack of nothing.

I Thessalonians 4:11, 12

Pray for us: for we trust we have a good conscience, in all things willing to live honestly.

Hebrews 13:18

Let integrity and uprightness preserve me; for I wait on thee.

Psalms 25:21

The just (man) walketh in his integrity: his children (are) blessed after him.

Proverbs 20:7

But sanctify the Lord God in your hearts: and (be) ready always to (give) and answer to every man that asketh you a reason of the hope that is in you with meekness and fear:

Having a good conscience; that, whereas they speak evil of you, as of evildoers, they may be ashamed that falsely accuse your good conversation in Christ.

For (it is) better, if the will of God be so, that ye suffer for well doing, than for evil doing.

I Peter 3:15-17

A false balance (is) abomination to the LORD: but a just weight (is) his delight.

Proverbs 11:1

Lying lips (are) abomination to the LORD: but they that deal truly (are) his delight.

Proverbs 12:22

A just weight and balance (are) the LORD'S: all the weights of the bag (are) his work.

Proverbs 16:11

Thou shalt not have in thy bag divers weights, a great and a small.

Thou shalt not have in thine house divers measures, a great and a small.

(But) thou shalt have a perfect and just weight, a perfect and just measure shalt thou have: that thy days may be lengthened in the land which the LORD thy God giveth thee.

For all that do such things, (and) all that do unrighteously, (are) an abomination unto the LORD thy God.

Deuteronomy 25:13-16

Finally, brethren, whatsoever things are true, whatsoever things (are) honest, whatsoever things (are) just, whatsoever things (are) pure, whatsoever things (are) lovely, whatsoever things (are) of good report; if (there be) any virtue and if (there be) any praise, think on these things.

Those things, which ye have both learned, and received, and heard, and seen in me, do: and the God of peace shall be with you.

Philippians 4:8, 9

Having therefore these promises, dearly beloved, let us cleanse ourselves from all filthiness of the flesh and spirit, perfecting holiness in the fear of God.

Receive us; we have wronged no man, we have corrupted no man, we have defrauded no man.

II Corinthians 7:1, 2

Having your conversation honest among the Gentiles: that, whereas they speak against you as evildoers, they may by (your) good works, which they shall behold, glorify God in the day of visitation.

I Peter 2:12

Thou shalt not steal.

Thou shalt not bear false witness against thy neighbour.

Thou shalt not covet thy neighbour's house, thou shalt not covet thy neighbour's wife, not his manservant, nor his maidservant, nor his ox, nor his ass, nor any thing that (is) thy neighbour's.

Exodus 20:15-17

Thou knowest the commandments, Do not commit adultery, Do not kill, Do not steal, Do not bear false witness, Defaud not, Honour thy father and mother.

Mark 10:19

Then came also publicans to be baptized, and said unto him, Master, what shall we do?

And he said unto them, Exact no more than that which is appointed you.

And the soldiers likewise demanded of him, saying, And what shall we do? And he said unto them, Do violence to no man, neither accuse (any) falsely; and be content with your wages.

Luke 3:12-14

And as ye would that men should do to you, do ye also to them likewise.

Luke 6:31

Let him that stole steal no more: but rather let him labour, working with (his) hands the thing which is good, that he may have to give to him that needeth.

Ephesians 4:28

Let not mercy and truth forsake thee: bind them about thy neck; write them upon the table of thine heart:

So shalt thou find favour and good understanding in the sight of God and man.

Proverbs 3:3, 4

A talebearer revealeth secrets: but he that is of a faithful spirit concealeth the matter.

Proverbs 11:13

Jesus saith unto her, Go, call thy husband, and come hither.

The woman answered and said, I have no husband. Jesus said unto her, Thou hast well said, I have no husband:

For thou hast had five husbands; and he whom thou now hast is not thy husband: in that saidst thou truly.

John 4:16-18

Ye shall not steal, neither deal falsely, neither lie one to another.

Leviticus 19:11

Thou shalt not go up and down (as) a talebearer among thy people: neither shalt thou stand against the blood of thy neighbour: I (am) the LORD.

Leviticus 19:16

These six (things) doth the LORD hate: yea, seven (are) an abomination unto him:

A proud look, a lying tongue, and hands that shed innocent blood,

An heart that deviseth wicked imaginations, feet that be swift in running mischief,

A false witness (that) speaketh lies, and he that soweth discord among brethren.

Proverbs 6:16-19

(He that) speaketh truth sheweth forth right-eousness: but a false witness deceit.

There is that speaketh like the piercings of a sword: but the tongue of the wise (is) health.

The lip of truth shall be established for ever: but a lying tongue (is) but for a moment.

Proverbs 12:17-19

Personnel Relations

Wherefore putting away lying, speak every man truth with his neighbour: for we are members one of another.

Be ye angry, and sin not: let not the sun go down upon your wrath:

Ephesians 4:25, 26

Let all bitterness, and wrath, and anger, and clamour, and evil speaking, be put away from you, with all malice:

And be ye kind one to another, tenderhearted, forgiving one another, even as God for Christ's sake hath forgiven you.

Ephesians 4:31, 32

(A Song of degrees of David.) Behold, how good and how pleasant (it is) for brethren to dwell together in unity!

Psalms 133:1

Now I beseech you, brethren, by the name of our Lord Jesus Christ, that ye all speak the same thing, and (that) there be no divisions among you; but (that) ye be perfectly joined together in the same mind and in the same judgment.

I Corinthians 1:10

Fulfil ye my joy, that ye be likeminded, having the same love, (being) of one accord, of one mind.

(Let) nothing (be done) through strife or vainglory; but in lowliness of mind let each esteem other better than themselves.

Look not every man on his own things, but every man also on the things of others.

Philippians 2:2-4

Ye have heard that it hath been said, An eye for an eye, and a tooth for a tooth:

But I say unto you, That ye resist not evil: but whosoever shall smite thee on thy right cheek, turn to him the other also.

And if any man will sue thee at the law, and take away thy coat, let him have (thy) cloke also.

And whosoever shall compel thee to go a mile, go with him twain.

Give to him that asketh thee, and from him that would borrow of thee turn not thou away.

Matthew 5:38-42

For if ye forgive men their trespasses, your heavenly Father will also forgive you:

But if ye forgive not men their trespasses, neither will your Father forgive your trespasses.

Matthew 6:14, 15

Judge not, that ye be not judged.

For with what judgment ye judge, ye shall be judged: and with what measure ye mete, it shall be measured to you again.

And why beholdest thou the mote that is in thy brother's eye, but considerest not the beam that is in thine own eye?

Or how wilt thou say to thy brother, Let me pull out the mote out of thine eye; and, behold, a beam (is) in thine own eye?

Thou hypocrite, first cast out the beam out of thine own eye; and then shalt thou see clearly to cast out the mote out of thy brother's eye.

Matthew 7:1-5

Therefore all things whatsoever ye would that men should do to you, do ye even so to them: for this is the law and the prophets.

Matthew 7:12

Blessed (are) the peacemakers: for they shall be called the children of God.

Matthew 5:9

But I say unto you, That whosoever is angry with his brother without a cause shall be in danger of the judgment: and whosoever shall say to his brother, Raca, shall be in danger of the council: but whosoever shall say, Thou fool, shall be in danger of hell fire.

Therefore if thou bring thy gift to the altar, and there rememberest that thy brother hath ought against thee;

Leave there thy gift before the altar, and go thy way; first be reconciled to thy brother, and then come and offer thy gift.

Matthew 5:22-24

For he taught them as (one) having authority, and not as the scribes.

Matthew 7:29

Ye have heard that it hath been said, Thou shalt love thy neighbour, and hate thine enemy.

But I say unto you, Love your enemies, bless them that curse you, do good to them that hate you, and pray for them which despitefully use you, and persecute you;

That ye may be the children of your Father which is in heaven; for he maketh his sun to rise on the evil and on the good, and sendeth rain on the just and on the unjust.

For if ye love them which love you, what reward have ye? do not even the publicans the same?

And if ye salute your brethren only, what do ye more (than others)? do not even the publicans so?

Be ye therefore perfect, even as your Father which is in heaven is perfect.

Matthew 5:43-48

Confess (your) faults one to another, and pray one for another, that ye may be healed. The effectual fervent prayer of a righteous man availeth much.

James 5:16

Forbearing one another, and forgiving one another, if any man have a quarrel against any: even as Christ forgave you, so also (do) ye.

Colossians 3:13

Let your speech (be) alway with grace, seasoned with salt, that ye may know how ye ought to answer every man.

Colossians 4:6

But now ye also put off all these; anger, wrath, malice, blasphemy, filthy communication out of your mouth.

Lie not one to another, seeing that ye have put off the old man with his deeds;

And have put on the new (man), which is renewed in knowledge after the image of him that created him:

Colossians 3:8-10

Charity suffereth long, (and) is kind; charity envieth not; charity vaunteth not itself, is not puffed up,

Doth not behave itself unseemly, seeketh not her own, is not easily provoked, thinketh no evil;

Rejoiceth not in inquity, but rejoiceth in the truth;

Beareth all things, believeth all things, hopeth all things, endureth all things.

I Corinthians 13:4-7

(Let) love be without dissimulation. Abhor that which is evil; cleave to that which is good.

(Be) kindly affectioned one to another with brotherly love; in honour preferrng one another;

Not slothful in business; fervent in spirit; serving the Lord;

Rejoicing in hope; patient in tribulation; continuing instant in prayer;

Distributing to the necessity of saints; given to hospitality.

Bless them which persecute you: bless, and curse not.

Rejoice with them that do rejoice, and weep with them that weep.

(Be) of the same mind one toward another. Mind not high things, but condescend to men of low estate. Be not wise in your own conceits.

Recompense to no man evil for evil. Provide things honest in the sight of all men.

If it be possible, as much as lieth in you, live peaceably with all men.

Dearly beloved, avenge not yourselves, but (rather) give place unto wrath: for it is written, Vengeance (is) mine; I will repay, saith the Lord.

Therefore if thine enemy hunger, feed him; if he thirst, give him drink: for in so doing thou shalt heap coals of fire on his head.

Be not overcome of evil, but overcome evil with good.

Romans 12:9-21

But if ye bite and devour one another, take heed that ye be not consumed one of another.

Galatians 5:15

Let us not be desirous of vain glory, provoking one another, envying one another.

Galatians 5:26

A talebearer revealeth secrets: but he that is of a faithful spirit concealeth the matter.

Proverbs 11:13

These six (things) doth the LORD hate: yea, seven (are) an abomination unto him:

A proud look, a lying tongue, and hands that shed innocent blood,

An heart that deviseth wicked imaginations, feet that be swift in running to mischief,

A false witness (that) speaketh lies, and he that soweth discord among brethren.

Proverbs 6:16-19

A merry heart maketh a cheerful countenance: but by sorrow of the heart the spirit is broken.

Proverbs 15:13

Pride (goeth) before destruction, and an haughty spirit before a fall.

Proverbs 16:18

Cast out the scorner, and contention shall go out; yea, strife and reproach shall cease.

Proverbs 22:10

Reward & Recognition

Every man's work shall be made manifest: for the day shall declare it, because it shall be revealed by fire; and the fire shall try every man's work of what sort it is.

If any man's work abide which he hath built thereupon, he shall receive a reward.

I Corinthians 3:13, 14

For though I preach the gospel, I have nothing to glory of: for necessity is laid upon me; yea, woe is unto me, if I preach not the gospel!

For if I do this thing willingly, I have a reward: but if against my will, a dispensation (of the gospel) is committed unto me.

What is my reward then? (Verily) that, when I preach the gospel, I may make the gospel of Christ without charge, that I abuse not my power in the gospel.

For though I be free from all (men), yet have I made myself servant unto all, that I might gain the more.

I Corinthians 9:16-19

Know ye not that they which run in a race run all, but one receiveth the prize? So run, that ye may obtain.

I Corinthians 9:24

And whatsoever ye do, do (it) heartily, as to the Lord, and not unto men;

Knowing that of the Lord ye shall receive the reward of the inheritance: for ye serve the Lord Christ.

Colossians 3:23, 24

He that receiveth a prophet in the name of a prophet shall receive a prophet's reward; and he that receiveth a righteous man in the name of a righteous man shall receive a righteous man's reward.

And whosoever shall give to drink unto one of these little ones a cup of cold (water) only in the name of a disciple, verily I say unto you, he shall in no wise lose his reward.

Matthew 10:41, 42

His lord said unto him, Well done, good and faithful servant; thou hast been faithful over a few things, I will make thee ruler over many things: enter thou into the joy of thy lord.

Matthew 25:23

Look to yourselves, that we lose not those things which we have wrought, but that we receive a full reward.

II John 1:8

He that hath an ear, let him hear what the Spirit saith unto the churches; To him that overcometh will I give to eat of the tree of life, which is in the midst of the paradise of God.

Revelation 2:7

Fear none of those things which thou shalt suffer: behold, the devil shall cast (some) of you into prison, that ye may be tried; and ye shall have tribulation ten days: be thou faithful unto death, and I will give thee a crown of life.

He that hath an ear, let him hear what the Spirit saith unto the churches; He that overcometh shall not be hurt of the second death.

Revelation 2:10, 11

He that hath an ear, let him hear what the Spirit saith unto the churches; To him that overcometh will I give to eat of the hidden manna, and will give him a white stone, and in the stone a new name written, which no man knoweth saving he that receiveth (it).

Revelation 2:17

And he that overcometh, and keepeth my works unto the end, to him will I give power over the nations:

Revelation 2:26

He that overcometh, the same shall be clothed in white raiment; and I will not blot out his name out of the book of life, but I will confess his name before my Father, and before his angels.

Revelation 3:5

Behold, I come quickly: hold that fast which thou hast, that no man take thy crown.

Him that overcometh will I make a pillar in the temple of my God, and he shall go no more out: and I will write upon him the name of my God, and the name of the city of my God, (which is) new Jerusalem, which cometh down out of heaven from my God: and (I will write upon him) my new name.

Revelaton 3:11, 12

For (God) giveth to a man that (is) good in his sight wisdom, and knowledge, and joy: but to the sinner he giveth travail, to gather and to heap up, that he may give to (him that is) good before God. This also (is) vanity and vexation of spirit.

Ecclesiastes 2:26

Cast thy bread upon the waters: for thou shalt find it after many days.

Ecclesiastes 11:1

But godliness with contentment is great gain.

For we brought nothing into (this) world, (and it is) certain we can carry nothing out.

And having food and raiment let us be therewith content.

I Timothy 6:6-8

Who then is Paul, and who (is) Apollos, but ministers by whom ye believed, even as the Lord gave to every man?

I have planted, Apollos watered; but God gave the increase.

So then neither is he that planteth any thing, neither he that watereth; but God that giveth the increase.

Now he that planteth and he that watereth are one: and every man shall receive his own reward according to his own labour.

For we are labourers together with God: ye are God's husbandry, (ye are) God's building.

I Corinthians 3:5-9

Correction & Discipline

My son, despise not the chastening of the LORD; neither be weary of his correction:

For whom the LORD loveth he correcteth; even as a father the son (in whom) he delighteth.

Proverbs 3:11, 12

He that spareth his rod hateth his son: but he that loveth him chasteneth him betimes.

Proverbs 13:24

A fool despiseth his father's instruction: but he that regardeth reproof is prudent.

Proverbs 15:5

Correction (is) grievous unto him that forsaketh the way: (and) he that hateth reproof shall die.

Proverbs 15:10

A scorner loveth not one that reproveth him: neither will he go unto the wise.

Proverbs 15:12

The ear that heareth the reproof of life abideth among the wise.

Proverbs 15:31

He that refuseth instruction despiseth his own soul: but he that heareth reproof getteth understanding.

Proverbs 15:32

And ye have forgotten the exhortation which speaketh unto you as unto children, My son, despise not thou the chastening of the Lord, nor faint when thou art rebuked of him:

For whom the Lord loveth he chasteneth, and scourgeth every son whom he receiveth.

If ye endure chastening, God dealeth with you as with sons; for what son is he whom the father chasteneth not?

But if ye be without chastisement, whereof all are partakers, then are ye bastards, and not sons.

Furthermore we have had fathers of our flesh which corrected (us), and we gave (them) reverence: shall we not much rather be in subjection unto the Father of spirits, and live?

For they verily for a few days chastened (us) after their own pleasure; but he for (our) profit, that (we) might be partakers of his holiness.

Now no chastening for the present seemeth to be joyous, but grievous: nevertheless afterward it yieldeth the peaceable fruit of righteousness unto them which are exercised thereby.

Hebrews 12:5-11

Then Peter said unto them, Repent, and be baptized every one of you in the name of Jesus Christ for the remission of sins, and ye shall receive the gift of the Holy Ghost.

Acts 2:38

Repent ye therefore, and be converted, that your sins may be blotted out, when the times of refreshing shall come from the presence of the Lord;

Acts 3:19

For all have sinned, and come short of the glory of God;

Romans 3:23

For the wages of sin (is) death; but the gift of God (is) eternal life through Jesus Christ our Lord.

Romans 6:23

All scripture (is) given by inspiration of God, and (is) profitable for doctrine, for reproof, for correction, for instruction in righteousness:

That the man of God may be perfect, throughly furnished unto all good works.

II Timothy 3:16, 17

And the Pharisees also, who were covetous, heard all these things: and they derided him.

And he said unto them, Ye are they which justify yourselves before men; but God knoweth your hearts: for that which is highly esteemed among men is abomination in the sight of God.

Luke 16:14, 15

Take heed to yourselves: If thy brothe₁ trespass against thee, rebuke him; and if he repent, forgive him.

And if he trespass against thee seven times in a day, and seven times in a day turn again to thee, saying, I repent; thou shalt forgive him.

Luke 17:3, 4

For every one that doeth evil hateth the light, neither cometh to the light, lest his deeds should be reproved.

But he that doeth truth cometh to the light, that his deeds may be made manifest, that they are wrought in God.

John 3:20, 21

Thou shalt not hate thy brother in thine heart: thou shalt in any wise rebuke thy neighbour, and not suffer sin upon him.

Leviticus 19:17

But ye, brethren, be not weary in well doing.

And if any man obey not our word by this epistle, note that man, and have no company with him, that he may be ashamed.

Yet count (him) not as an enemy, but admonish (him) as a brother.

II Thessalonians 3:13-15

He that reproveth a scorner getteth to himself shame: and he that rebuketh a wicked (man getteth) himself a blot.

Reprove not a scourner, lest he hate thee: rebuke a wise man, and he will love thee.

Proverbs 9:7, 8

The rod and reproof give wisdom: but a child left (to himself) bringeth his mother to shame.

Correct thy son, and he shall give thee rest; yea, he shall give delight unto thy soul.

Proverbs 29:15, 17

Negotiation

(He that is) slow to wrath (is) of great understanding: but (he that is) hasty of spirit exalteth folly.

Proverbs 14:29

He that hath knowledge spareth his words: (and) a man of understanding is of an excellent spirit.

Proverbs 17:27

He that goeth about (as) a talebearer revealeth secrets: therefore meddle not with him that flattereth with his lips.

Proverbs 20:19

Better (is) the end of a thing than the beginning thereof: (and) the patient in spirit (is) better than the proud in spirit.

Ecclesiastes 7:8

A wholesome tongue (is) a tree of life: but perverseness therein (is) a breach in the spirit.

Proverbs 15:4

He that handleth a matter wisely shall find good: and whoso trusteth in the LORD, happy (is) he.

Proverbs 16:20

Better (it is to be) of an humble spirit with the lowly, than to divide the spoil with the proud.

Proverbs 16:19

And Abram said unto Lot, Let there be no strife, I pray thee, between me and thee, and between my herdmen and thy herdmen; for we (be) brethren.

(Is) not the whole land before thee? separate thyself, I pray thee, from me: if (thou wilt take) the left hand, then I will go to the right; or if (thou depart) to the right hand, then I will go to the left.

And Lot lifted up his eyes, and beheld all the plain of Jordan, that it (was) well watered every where, before the LORD destroyed Sodom and Gomorrah, (even) as the garden of the LORD, like the land of Egypt, as thou comest unto Zoar.

Genesis 13:8-10

And Laban said unto Jacob, Because thou (art) my brother, shouldest thou therefore serve me for nought? tell me, what (shall) thy wages (be)?

And Laban had two daughters: the name of the elder (was) Leah, and the name of the younger (was) Rachel.

Leah (was) tender eyed; but Rachel was beautiful and well favoured.

And Jacob loved Rachel; and said, I will serve thee seven years for Rachel thy younger daugther.

And Laban said, (It is) better that I give her to thee, than that I should give her to another man: abide with me.

And Jacob served seven years for Rachel; and they seemed unto him (but) a few days, for the love he had to her.

Genesis 29:15-20

And Joseph said unto his brethren, and unto his father's house, I will go up, and shew Pharaoh, and say unto him, My brethren, and my father's house, which (were) in the land of Canaan, are come unto me;

And the men (are) shepherds, for their trade hath been to feed cattle; and they have brought their flocks, and their herds, and all that they have.

And it shall come to pass, when Pharaoh shall call you, and shall say, What (is) your occupation?

That ye shall say, Thy servants' trade hath been about cattle from our youth even until now, both we, (and) also our fathers: that ye may dwell in the land of Goshen; for every shepherd (is) an abomination unto the Egyptians.

Genesis 46:31-34

And (there was) no bread in all the land; for the famine (was) very sore, so that the land of Egypt and (all) the land of Canaan fainted by reason of the famine.

And Joseph gathered up all the money that was found in the land of Egypt, and in the land of Canaan, for the corn which they bought: and Joseph brought the money into Pharaoh's house.

And when money failed in the land of Egypt, and in the land of Canaan, all the Egyptians came unto Joseph, and said, Give us bread: for why should we die in thy presence? for the money faileth.

And Joseph said, Give your cattle; and I will give you for your cattle, if money fail.

And they brought their cattle unto Joseph: and Joseph gave them bread (in exchange) for horses, and for the flocks, and for the cattle of the herds, and for the asses: and he fed them with bread for all their cattle for that year.

Genesis 47:13-17

Come now therefore, and I will send thee unto Pharaoh, that thou mayest bring forth my people the children of Israel out of Egypt.

And Moses said unto God, Who (am) I, that I should go unto Pharaoh, and that I should bring forth the children of Israel out of Egypt?

And he said, Certainly I will be with thee; and this (shall be) a token unto thee, that I have sent thee: When thou hast brought forth the people out of Egypt, ye shall serve God upon this mountain.

And Moses said unto God, Behold, (when) I come unto the children of Israel, and shall say unto them, The God of your fathers hath sent me unto you; and they shall say to me, What (is) his name? what shall I say unto them?

And God said unto Moses, I AM THAT I AM: and he said, Thus shalt thou say unto the children of Israel, I AM hath sent me unto you.

Exodus 3:10-14

And Moses said unto the LORD, O my Lord, I (am) not eloquent, neither heretofore, nor since thou hast spoken unto they servant: but I (am) slow of speech, and of a slow tongue.

And the LORD said unto him, Who hath made man's mouth? or who maketh the dumb, or deaf, or the seeing, or the blind? have not I the LORD?

Now therefore go, and I will be with thy mouth, and teach thee what thou shalt say.

And he said, O my Lord, send, I pray thee, by the hand (of him whom) thou wilt send.

And the anger of the LORD was kindled against Moses, and he said, (Is) not Aaron the Levite thy brother? I know that he can speak well. And also, behold, he cometh forth to meet thee: and when he seeth thee, he will be glad in his heart.

Exodus 4:10-14

Therefore the people came to Moses, and said, We have sinned, for we have spoken against the LORD, and against thee; pray unto the LORD, that he take away the serpents from us. And Moses prayed for the people.

Numbers 21:7

And Jesus being full of the Holy Ghost returned from Jordan, and was led by the Spirit into the wilderness,

Being forty days tempted of the devil. And in those days he did eat nothing: and when they were ended, he afterward hungered.

And the devil said unto him, If thou be the Son of God, command this stone that it be made bread.

And Jesus answered him, saying, It is written, That man shall not live by bread alone, but by every word of God.

And the devil, taking him up into a high mountain, shewed unto him all the kingdoms of the world in a moment of time.

And the devil said unto him, All this power will I give thee, and the glory of them: for that is delivered unto me; and to whomsoever I will I give it.

If thou therefore wilt worship me, all shall be thine.

And Jesus answered and said unto him, Get thee behind me, Satan: for it is written, Thou shalt worship the Lord thy God, and him only shalt thou serve.

And ne brought him to Jerusalem, and set him on a pinnacle of the temple, and said unto him, If thou be the Son of God, cast thyself down from hence:

For it is written, He shall give his angels charge over thee, to keep thee:

And in (their) hands they shall bear thee up, lest at any time thou dash thy foot against a stone.

And Jesus answering said unto him, It is said, Thou shalt not tempt the Lord thy God.

And when the devil had ended all the temptation, he departed from him for a season.

Luke 4:1-13

And it came to pass, when he was come nigh to Bethphage and Bethany, at the mount called (the mount) of Olives, he sent two of his disciples,

Saying, Go ye into the village over against (you); in the which at your entering ye shall find a colt tied, whereon yet never man sat: loose him, and bring (him hither).

And if any man ask you, Why do ye loose (him)? thus shall ye say unto him, Because the Lord hath need of him.

And they that were sent went their way, and found even as he had said unto them.

And as they were loosing the colt, the owners thereof said unto them, Why loose ye the colt?

And they said, The Lord hath need of him.

Luke 19:29-34

Debate thy cause with thy neighbour (himself); and discover not a secret to another:

Lest he that heareth (it) put thee to shame, and thine infamy turn not away.

Proverbs 25:9, 10

Let your speech (be) alway with grace, seasoned with salt, that ye may know how ye ought to answer every man.

Colossians 4:6

Charitableness & Generosity

Though I speak with the tongues of men and of angels, and have not charity, I am become (as) sounding brass, or a tinkling cymbal.

And though I have (the gift of) prophecy, and understand all mysteries, and all knowledge; and though I have all faith, so that I could remove mountains, and have not charity, I am nothing.

And though I bestow all my goods to feed (the poor), and though I give my body to be burned, and have not charity, it profiteth me nothing.

Charity suffereth long, (and) is kind; charity envieth not; charity vaunteth not itself, is not puffed up,

Doth not behave itself unseemly, seeketh not her own, is not easily provoked, thinketh no evil;

Rejoiceth not in iniquity, but rejoiceth in the truth;

Beareth all things, believeth all things, hopeth all things, endureth all things.

Charity never faileth: but whether (there be) prophecies, they shall fail; whether (there be) tongues, they shall cease; whether (there be) knowledge, it shall vanish away.

For we know in part, and we prophesy in part.

But when that which is perfect is come, then that which is in part shall be done away.

When I was a child, I spake as a child, I understood as a child, I thought as a child: but when I became a man, I put away childish things.

For now we see through a glass, darkly; but then face to face: now I know in part; but then shall I know even as also I am known.

And now abideth faith, hope, charity, these three; but the greatest of these (is) charity.

I Corinthians 13:1-13

Master, which (is) the great commandment in the law?

Jesus said unto him, Thou shalt love the Lord thy God with all thy heart, and with all thy soul, and with all thy mind.

This is the first and great commandment.

And the second (is) like unto it, Thou shalt love thy neighbour as thyself.

Matthew 22:36-39

But a certain Samaritan, as he journeyed, came where he was: and when he saw him, he had compassion (on him),

And went to (him), and bound up his wounds, pouring in oil and wine, and set him on his own beast, and brought him to an inn, and took care of him.

And on the morrow when he departed, he took out two pence, and gave (them) to the host, and said unto him, Take care of him; and whatsoever thou spendest more, when I come again, I will repay thee.

Luke 10:33-35

This is my commandment, That ye love one another, as I have loved you.

Greater love hath no man than this, that a man lay down his life for his friends.

John 15:12, 13

When the Son of man shall come in his glory, and all the holy angels with him, then shall he sit upon the throne of glory:

And before him shall be gathered all nations: and he shall separate them one from another, as a shepherd divideth (his) sheep from the goats:

And he shall set the sheep on his right hand, but the goats on the left.

Then shall the King say unto them on his right hand, Come, ye blessed of my Father, inherit the kindom prepared for you from the foundation of the world:

For I was an hungred, and ye gave me meat: I was thirsty, and ye gave me drink: I was a stranger, and ye took me in:

Naked, and ye clothed me: I was sick, and ye visited me: I was in prison, and ye came unto me.

Then shall the righteous answer him, saying, Lord, when saw we thee an hungred, and fed (thee)? or thirsty, and gave (thee) drink?

When saw we thee a stranger, and took (thee) in? or naked, and clothed (thee)?

Or when saw we thee sick, or in prison, and came unto thee?

And the King shall answer and say unto them, Verily I say unto you, Inasmuch as ye have done (it) unto one of the least of these my brethren, ye have done (it) unto me.

Matthew 25:31-40

Bring ye all the tithes into the storehouse, that there may be meant in mine house, and prove me now herewith, saith the LORD of hosts, if I will not open you the windows of heaven, and pour you out a blessing, that (there shall) not (be room) enough (to receive it).

Malachi 3:10

And he looked up, and saw the rich men casting their gifts into the treasury.

And he saw also a certain poor widow casting in thither two mites.

And he said, Of a truth I say unto you, that this poor widow hath cast in more than they all:

For all these have of their abundance cast in unto the offerings of God: but she of her penury hath cast in all the living that she had.

Luke 21:1-4

Give, and it shall be given unto you; good measure; pressed down, and shaken together, and running over, shall men give into your bosom. For with the same measure that ye mete withal it shall be measured to you again.

Luke 6:38

Every man according as he purposeth in his heart, (so let him give); not grudgingly, or of necessity: for God loveth a cheerful giver.

II Corinthians 9:7

Now when Jesus was in Bethany, in the house of Simon the leper,

There came unto him a woman having an alabaster box of very precious ointment, and poured it on his head, as he sat (at meat).

But when his disciples saw (it), they had indignation, saying, To what purpose (is) this waste?

For this ointment might have been sold for much, and given to the poor.

When Jesus understood (it), he said unto them, Why trouble ye the woman? for she hath wrought a good work upon me.

For ye have the poor always with you; but me ye have not always.

For in that she hath poured this ointment on my body, she did (it) for my burial.

Verily I say unto you, Wheresoever this gospel shall be preached in the whole world, (there) shall also this, that this woman hath done, be told for a memorial of her.

Matthew 26:6-13

But this (I say), He which soweth sparingly shall reap also sparingly; and he which soweth bountifully shall reap also bountifully.

II Corinthians 9:6

Honour the LORD with thy substance, and with the firstfruits of all thine increase:

Proverbs 3:9

Every man (shall give) as he is able, according to the blessing of the LORD thy God which he hath given thee.

Deuteronomy 16:17

Upon the first (day) of the week let every one of you lay by him in store, as (God) hath prospered him, that there be no gatherings when I come.

I Corinthians 16:2

But the end of all things is at hand: be ye therefore sober, and watch unto prayer.

And above all things have fervent charity among yourselves: for charity shall cover the multitude of sins.

Use hospitality one to another without grudging.

As every man hath received the gift, (even so) minister the same one to another, as good stewards of the manifold grace of God.

I Peter 4:7-10

We then that are strong ought to bear the infirmities of the weak, and not to please ourselves.

Let every one of us please (his) neighbour for (his) good to edification.

Wherefore receive ye one another, as Christ also received us to the glory of God.

Romans 15:1, 2, 7

Then the disciples, every man according to his ability, determined to send relief unto the brethren which dwelt in Judaea:

Acts 11:29

Brethren, if a man be overtaken in a fault, ye which are spiritual, restore such an one in the spirit of meekness; considering thyself, lest thou also be tempted.

Galatians 6:1

Give to him that asketh thee, and from him that would borrow of thee turn not thou away.

Matthew 5:42

If thine enemy be hungry, give him bread to eat; and if he be thirsty, give him water to drink:

Proverbs 25:21

I have shewed you all things, how that so labouring ye ought to support the weak, and to remember the words of the Lord Jesus, how he said, It is more blessed to give than to receive.

Acts 20:35

He that hath a bountiful eye shall be blessed; for he giveth of his bread to the poor.

Proverbs 22:9

And when they had prayed, the place was shaken where they were assembled together; and they were all filled with the Holy Ghost, and they spake the word of God with boldness.

And the multitude of them that believed were of one heart and of one soul: neither said any (of them) that ought of the things which he possessed was his own; but they had all things common.

And with great power gave the apostles witness of the resurrection of the Lord Jesus: and great grace was upon them all.

Neither was there any among them that lacked: for as many as were possessors of lands or houses sold them, and brought the prices of the things that were sold,

And laid (them) down at the apostles' feet: and distribution was made unto every man according as he had need.

Acts 4:31-35

(Is it) not to deal thy bread to the hungry, and that thou bring the poor that are cast out to thy house? when thou seest the naked, that thou cover him; and that thou hide not thyself from thine own flesh?

And (if) thou draw out thy soul to the hungry, and satisfy the afflicted soul; then shall thy light rise in obscurity, and thy darkness (be) as the noon day:

Woe unto them that rise up early in the morning, (that) they may follow strong drink; that continue until night, (till) wine inflame them!

Isaiah 58:7, 10, 11

Whoso stoppeth his ears at the cry of the poor, he also shall cry himself, but shall not be heard.

Proverbs 21:13

Heal the sick, cleanse the lepers, raise the dead, cast out devils: freely ye have received, freely give.

Matthew 10:8

But when thou doest alms, let not thy left hand know what thy right hand doeth:

That thine alms may be in secret: and thy Father which seeth in secret himself shall reward thee openly.

Matthew 6:3, 4

So we, (being) many, are one body in Christ, and every one members one of another.

Having then gifts differing according to the grace that is given to us, whether prophecy, (let us prophesy) according to the proportion of faith;

Or he that exhorteth on exhortation: he that giveth, (let him do it) with simplicity; he that ruleth, with diligence; he that sheweth mercy, with cheerfulness.

Romans 12:5, 6, 8

And they came, both men and women, as many as were willing hearted, (and) brought bracelets, and earrings, and rings, and tablets, all jewels of gold: and every man that offered (offered) an offering of gold unto the LORD.

Exodus 35:22

And they brought their offering before the LORD, six covered wagons, and twelve oxen; a wagon for two of the princes, and for each one an ox: and they brought them before the tabernacle.

Numbers 7:3

And the men which were expressed by name rose up, and took the captives, and with the spoil clothed all that were naked among them, and arrayed them, and shod them, and gave them to eat and to drink, and anointed them, and carried all the feeble of them upon asses, and brought them to Jericho, the city of palm trees, to their brethren: then they return-ed to Samaria.

II Chronicles 28:15

Cast thy bread upon the waters: for thou shalt find it after many days.

Ecclesiastes 11:1

The liberal soul shall be made fat: and he that watereth shall be watered also himself.

Proverbs 11:25

Biblical Counsel For Trying Times In Your Business...

Handling Stress & Pressure

Come unto me, all (ye) that labour and are
heavy laden, and I will give you rest.

Take my yoke upon you, and learn of me;
for I am meek and lowly in heart: and ye shall find
rest unto your souls.

For my yoke (is) easy, and my burden is
light.

Matthew 11:28-30

Casting all your care upon him; for he
careth for you.

I Peter 5:7

Thus the heavens and the earth were finished, and all the host of them.

And on the seventh day God ended his work
which he had made; and he rested on the seventh
day from all his work which he had made.

And God blessed the seventh day, and sanc-
tified it: because that in it he had rested from all
his work which God created and made.

Genesis 2:1-3

And Moses said unto the LORD, See, thou
sayest unto me, Bring up this people: and thou hast
not let me know whom thou wilt send with me.
Yet thou hast said, I know thee by name, and thou
hast also found grace in my sight.

Now therefore, I pray thee, if I have found grace in thy sight, shew me now thy way, that I may know thee, that I may find grace in thy sight: and consider that this nation (is) thy people.

And he said, My presence shall go (with thee), and I will give thee rest.

Exodus 33:12-14

There hath no temptation taken you but such as is common to man: but God (is) faithful, who will not suffer you to be tempted above that ye are able; but will with the temptation also make a way to escape, that ye may be able to bear (it).

I Corinthians 10:13

Heaviness in the heart of man maketh it stoop: but a good word maketh it glad.

Proverbs 12:25

Let your light so shine before men, that they may see your good works, and glorify your Father which is in heaven.

Matthew 5:16

A good man out of the good treasure of his heart bringeth forth that which is good; and an evil man out of the evil treasure of his heart bringeth forth that which is evil: for of the abundance of the heart his mouth speaketh.

Luke 6:45

(He that is) slow to wrath (is) of great understanding: but (he that is) hasty of spirit exalteth folly.

Proverbs 14:29

(He that is) slow to anger (is) better than the mighty; and he that ruleth his spirit than he that taketh a city.

Proverbs 16:32

Go thy way, eat thy bread with joy, and drink thy wine with a merry heart; for God now accepteth thy works.

Let thy garments be always white; and let thy head lack no ointment.

Live joyfully with the wife whom thou lovest all the days of the life of thy vanity, which he hath given thee under the sun, all the days of thy vanity: for that (is) thy portion in (this) life, and in thy labour which thou takest under the sun.

Ecclesiastes 9: 7-9

(A Song of degrees.) I will lift up mine eyes unto the hills, from whence cometh my help.

My help (cometh) from the LORD, which made heaven and earth.

He will not suffer thy foot to be moved: he that keepeth thee will not slumber.

Behold, he that keepeth Israel shall neither slumber nor sleep.

The LORD (is) thy keeper: the LORD (is) thy shade upon thy right hand.

The sun shall not smite thee by day, nor the moon by night.

The LORD shall preserve thee from all evil: he shall preserve thy soul.

The LORD shall preserve thy going out and thy coming in from this time forth, and even for evermore.

Psalms 121:1-8

In every thing give thanks: for this is the will of God in Christ Jesus concerning you.

I Thessalonians 5:18

Be careful for nothing; but in every thing by prayer and supplication with thanksgiving let your requests be made known unto God.

And the peace of God, which passeth all understanding, shall keep your hearts and minds through Christ Jesus.

Philippians 4:6, 7

Peace I leave with you, my peace I give unto you: not as the world giveth, give I unto you. Let not your heart be troubled, neither let it be afraid.

Ye have heard how I said unto you, I go away, and come (again) unto you. If ye loved me, ye would rejoice, because I said, I go unto the Father: for my Father is greater than I.

John 14:27, 28

Hungry and thirsty, their soul fainted in them.

Then they cried unto the LORD in their trouble, (and) he delivered them out of their distresses.

And he led them forth by the right way, that they might go to a city of habitation.

Psalms 107:5-7

Surley he shall deliver thee from the snare of the fowler, (and) from the noisome pestilence.

He shall cover thee with his feathers, and under his wings shalt thou trust: his truth (shall be thy) shield and buckler.

Thou shalt not be afraid for the terror by night; (nor) for the arrow (that) flieth by day;

(Nor) for the pestilence (that) walketh in darkness; (nor) for the destruction (that) wasteth at noonday.

A thousand shall fall at thy side, and ten thousand at thy right hand; (but) it shall not come nigh thee.

Psalms 91:3-7

(To the chief Musician for the sons of Korah, A Song upon Alamoth.) God (is) our refuge and strength, a very present help in trouble.

Therefore will not we fear, though the earth be removed, and though the mountains be carried into the midst of the sea;

(Though) the waters thereof roar (and) be troubled, (though) the mountains shake with the swelling thereof. Selah.

Psalms 46:1-3

The LORD also will be a refuge for the oppressed, a refuge in times of trouble.

And they that know thy name will put their trust in thee: for thou, LORD, hast not forsaken them that seek thee.

Psalms 9:9, 10

Overcoming Obstacles & Difficulties

Nay, in all these things we are more than conquerors through him that loved us.

For I am persuaded, that neither death, nor life, nor angels, nor principalities, nor powers, nor things present, nor things to come,

Nor height, nor depth, nor any other creature, shall be able to separate us from the love of God, which is in Christ Jesus our Lord.

Romans 8:37-39

Beloved, think it not strange concerning the fiery trial which is to try you, as though some strange thing happened unto you:

But rejoice, inasmuch as ye are partakers of Christ's sufferings; that, when his glory shall be revealed, ye may be glad also with exceeding joy.

If ye be reproached for the name of Christ, happy are ye; for the spirit of glory and of God resteth upon you: on their part he is evil spoken of, but on your part he is glorified.

Yet if any man suffer as a Christian, let him not be ashamed; but let him glorify God on this behalf.

I Peter 4:12-14, 16

And not only (so), but we glory in tribulations also: knowing that tribulation worketh patience;

And patience, experience; and experience, hope:

And hope maketh not ashamed; because the love of God is shed abroad in our hearts by the Holy Ghost which is given unto us.

Romans 5:3-5

Likewise the Spirit also helpeth our infirmities: for we know not what we should pray for as we ought: but the Spirit itself maketh intercession for us with groanings which cannot be uttered.

Romans 8:26

For this thing I besought the Lord thrice, that it might depart from me.

And he said unto me, My grace is sufficient for thee: for my strength is made perfect in weakness. Most gladly therefore will I rather glory in my infirmities, that the power of Christ may rest upon me.

Therefore I take pleasure in infirmities, in reproaches, in necessities, in persecutions, in distresses for Christ's sake: for when I am weak, then am I strong.

II Corinthians 12:8-10

(To the chief Musician upon Jonath-elem-rechokim, Michtam of David, when the Philistines took him in Gath.) Be merciful unto me, O God: for man would swallow me up; he fighting daily oppresseth me.

Mine enemies would daily swallow (me) up: for (they be) many that fight against me, O thou most High.

What time I am afraid, I will trust in thee.

In God I will praise his word, in God I have put my trust; I will not fear what flesh can do unto me.

Psalms 56:1-4

My brethren, count it all joy when ye fall into divers temptations;

Knowing (this), that the trying of your faith worketh patience.

But let patience have (her) perfect work, that ye may be perfect and entire, wanting nothing.

James 1:2-4

Then said he unto the disciples, It is impossible but that offences will come: but woe (unto him), through whom they come!

It were better for him that a millstone were hanged about his neck, and he cast into the sea, than that he should offend one of these little ones.

Luke 17:1, 2

There shall no evil befall thee, neither shall any plague come nigh thy dwelling.

For he shall give his angels charge over thee, to keep thee in all thy ways.

They shall bear thee up in (their) hands, lest thou dash thy foot against a stone.

Thou shalt tread upon the lion and adder: the young lion and the dragon shalt thou trample under feet.

Because he hath set his love upon me, therefore will I deliver him: I will set him on high, because he hath known my name.

He shall call upon me, and I will answer him: I (will be) with him in trouble; I will deliver him, and honour him.

With long life will I satisfy him, and shew him my salvation.

Psalms 91:10-16

For the kingdom of God is not meat and drink; but righteousness, and peace, and joy in the Holy Ghost.

For he that in these things serveth Christ (is) acceptable to God and approved of men.

Let us therefore follow after the things which make for peace, and things wherewith one may edify another.

Romans 14:17-19

Delight thyself also in the LORD; and he shall give thee the desires of thine heart.

Commit thy way unto the LORD; trust also in him; and he shall bring (it) to pass.

Psalms 37:4, 5

Behold, the eye of the LORD (is) upon them that fear him, upon them that hope in his mercy;

To deliver their soul from death, and to keep them alive in famine.

Our soul waiteth for the LORD: he (is) our help and our shield.

For our heart shall rejoice in him, because we have trusted in his holy name.

Let thy mercy, O LORD, be upon us, according as we hope in thee.

Psalms 33:18-22

One man of you shall chase a thousand: for the LORD your God, he (it is) that fighteth for you, as he hath promised you.

Take good heed therefore unto yourselves, that ye love the LORD your God.

Joshua 23:10, 11

And call upon me in the day of trouble: I will deliver thee, and thou shalt glorify me.

Psalms 50:15

A Positive Attitude

Be careful for nothing; but in every thing
by prayer and supplication with thanksgiving let
your requests be made known unto God.

Philippians 4:6

Jesus said unto him, If thou canst believe,
all things (are) possible to him that believeth.

Mark 9:23

As in water face (answereth) to face, so the
heart of man to man.

Proverbs 27:19

For as he thinketh in his heart, so (is) he:
Eat and drink, saith he to thee; but his heart (is) not
with thee.

Proverbs 23:7

Cast not away therefore your confidence,
which hath great recompence of reward.

Hebrews 10:35

And Caleb stilled the people before Moses,
and said, Let us go up at once, and possess it; for
we are well able to overcome it.

But the men that went up with him said,
We be not able to go up against the people; for
they (are) stronger than we.

And there we saw the giants, the sons of Anak, (which come) of the giants: and we were in our own sight as grasshoppers, and so we were in their sight.

Numbers 13:30, 31, 33

Come now therefore, and I will send thee unto Pharaoh, that thou mayest bring forth my people the children of Israel out of Egypt.

And Moses said unto God, Who (am) I, that I should go unto Pharaoh, and that I should bring forth the children of Israel out of Egypt?

And he said, Certainly I will be with thee; and this (shall be) a token unto thee, that I have sent thee: When thou hast brought forth the people out of Egypt, ye shall serve God upon this mountain.

Exodus 3:10-12

I can do all things through Christ which strengtheneth me.

Philippians 4:13

Wherefore lift up the hands which hang down, and the feeble knees;

And make straight paths for your feet, lest that which is lame be turned out of the way; but let it rather be healed.

Hebrews 12:12, 13

Blessed (is) the man that trusteth in the LORD, and whose hope the LORD is.

For he shall be as a tree planted by the waters, and (that) spreadeth out her roots by the river, and shall not see when heat cometh, but her leaf shall be green; and shall not be careful in the year of drought, neither shall cease from yielding fruit.

Jeremiah 17:7, 8

And the Lord said, If ye had faith as a grain of mustard seed, ye might say unto this sycamine tree, Be thou plucked up by the root, and be thou planted in the sea; and it should obey you.

Luke 17:6

Finally, brethren, whatsoever things are true, whatsoever things (are) honest, whatsoever things (are) just, whatsoever things (are) pure, whatsoever things (are) lovely, whatsoever things (are) of good report; if (there be) any virtue, and if (there be) any praise, think on these things.

Those things, which ye have both learned, and received, and heard, and seen in me, do: and the God of peace shall be with you.

Philippians 4:8, 9

Now the God of hope fill you with all joy and peace in believing, that ye may abound in hope, through the power of the Holy Ghost.

Romans 15:13

And David said to Saul, Let no man's heart fail because of hom; thy servant will go and fight with this Philistine.

And Saul said to David, Thou art not able to go against this Philistine to fight with him: for thou (art but) a youth, and he a man of war from his youth.

And David said unto Saul, Thy servant kept his father's sheep, and there came a lion, and a bear, and took a lamb out of the flock:

And I went out after him, and smote him, and delivered (it) out of his mouth: and when he arose against me, I caught (him) by his beard, and smote him, and slew him.

Thy servant slew both the lion and the bear: and this uncircumcised Philistine shall be as one of them, seeing he hath defied the armies of the living God.

I Samuel 17:32-36

But the ship was now in the midst of the sea, tossed with waves: for the wind was contrary.

And in the fourth watch of the night Jesus went unto them, walking on the sea.

And when the disciples saw him walking on the sea, they were troubled, saying, It is a spirit; and they cried out for fear.

But straightway Jesus spake unto them, saying, Be of good cheer; it is I; be not afraid.

And Peter answered him and said, Lord, if it be thou, bid me come unto thee on the water.

And he said, Come. And when Peter was come down out of the ship, he walked on the water, to go to Jesus.

But when he saw the wind boisterous, he was afraid; and beginning to sink, he cried, saying, Lord, save me.

And immediately Jesus stretched forth (his) hand, and caught him, and said unto him, O thou of little faith, wherefore didst thou doubt?

And when they were come into the ship, the wind ceased.

Then they that were in the ship came and worshipped him, saying, Of a truth thou art the Son of God.

Matthew 14:24–33

But let all those that put their trust in thee rejoice: let them ever shout for joy, because thou defendest them: let them also that love thy name be joyful in thee.

Psalms 5:11

A good man sheweth favour, and lendeth: he will guide his affairs with discretion.

Surely he shall not be moved for ever: the righteous shall be in everlasting remembrance.

He shall not be afraid of evil tidings: his heart is fixed, trusting in the LORD.

His heart (is) established, he shall not be afraid, until he see (his desire) upon his enemies.

Psalms 112:5-8

Thou wilt keep (him) in perfect peace, (whose) mind (is) stayed (on thee): because he trusteth in thee.

Isaiah 26:3

How excellent (is) thy lovingkindness, O God! therefore the children of men put their trust under the shadow of thy wings.

Psalms 36:7

Blessed (is) the man that trusteth in the LORD, and whose hope the LORD is.

For he shall be as a tree planted by the waters, and (that) spreadeth out her roots by the river, and shall not see when heat cometh, but her leaf shall be green; and shall not be careful in the year of drought, neither shall cease from yielding fruit.

Jeremiah 17:7, 8

I have fought a good fight, I have finished (my) course, I have kept the faith:

Henceforth there is laid up for me a crown of righteousness, which the Lord, the righteous judge, shall give me at that day: and not to me only, but unto all them also that love his appearing.

II Timothy 4:7, 8

Now faith is the substance of things hoped for, the evidence of things not seen.

For by it the elders obtained a good report.

Through faith we understand that the worlds were framed by the word of God, so that things which are seen were not made of things which do appear.

By faith Abel offered unto God a more excellent sacrifice than Cain, by which he obtained witness that he was righteous, God testifying of his gifts: and by it he being dead yet speaketh.

By faith Enoch was translated that he should not see death; and was not found, because God had translated him: for before his translation he had this testimony, that he pleased God.

But without faith (it is) impossible to please (him): for he that cometh to God must believe that he is, and (that) he is a rewarder of them that diligently seek him.

Hebrews 11:1-6

But be ye doers of the word, and not hearers only, deceiving your own selves.

For if any be a hearer of the word, and not a doer, he is like unto a man beholding his natural face in a glass:

For he beholdeth himself, and goeth his way, and straightway forgetteth what manner of man he was.

James 1:22-24

For whatsoever is born of God overcometh the world: and this is the victory that overcometh the world, (even) our faith.

I John 5:4

When thou goest out to battle against thine enemies, and seest horses, and chariots, (and) a people more than thou, be not afraid of them: for the Lord thy God (is) with thee, which brought thee up out of the land of Egypt.

Deuteronomy 20:1

For the eyes of the LORD run to and fro throughout the whole earth, to shew himself strong in the behalf of (them) whose heart (is) perfect toward him. Herein thou hast done foolishly: therefore from henceforth thou shalt have wars.

II Chronicles 16:9

And one of them, when he saw that he was healed, turned back, and with a loud voice glorified God,

And fell down on (his) face at his feet, giving him thanks: and he was a Samaritan.

Luke 17:15, 16

In every thing give thanks: for this is the will of God in Christ Jesus concerning you.

I Thessalonians 5:18

Saying, What wilt thou that I shall do unto thee? And he said, Lord, that I may receive my sight.

And Jesus said unto him, Receive thy sight: thy faith hath saved thee.

And immediately he received his sight, and followed him, glorifying God: and all the people, when they saw (it), gave praise unto God.

Luke 18:41-43

In Crisis Situations

(We are) troubled on every side, yet not distressed; (we are) perplexed, but not in despair;

Persecuted, but not forsaken; cast down, but not destroyed;

II Corinthians 4:8, 9

Though I walk in the midst of trouble, thou wilt revive me: thou shalt stretch forth thine hand against the wrath of mine enemies, and thy right hand shall save me.

Psalms 138:7

Take therefore no thought for the morrow: for the morrow shall take thought for the things of itself. Sufficient unto the day (is) the evil thereof.

Matthew 6:34

Be careful for nothing; but in every thing by prayer and supplication with thanksgiving let your requests be made known unto God.

And the peace of God, which passeth all understanding, shall keep your hearts and minds through Christ Jesus.

Philippians 4:6, 7

And we know that all things work together for good to them that love God, to them who are the called according to (his) purpose.

Romans 8:28

For we have not an high priest which cannot be touched with the feeling of our infirmities; but was in all points tempted like as (we are, yet) without sin.

Let us therefore come boldly unto the throne of grace, that we may obtain mercy, and find grace to help in time of need.

Hebrews 4:15, 16

The LORD (is) good, a strong hold in the day of trouble; and he knoweth them that trust in him.

Nahum 1:7

Blessed (be) God, even the Father of our Lord Jesus Christ, the Father of mercies, and the God of all comfort;

Who comforteth us in all our tribulation, that we may be able to comfort them which are in any trouble, by the comfort wherewith we ourselves are comforted of God.

II Corinthians 1:3, 4

Beloved, think it not strange concerning the fiery trial which is to try you, as though some strange thing happened unto you:

But rejoice, inasmuch as ye are partakers of Christ's sufferings; that, when his glory shall be revealed, ye may be glad also with exceeding joy.

I Peter 4:12, 13

But my God shall supply all your need according to his riches in glory by Christ Jesus.

Philippians 4:19

Because he hath set his love upon me, therefore will I deliver him: I will set him on high, because he hath known my name.

He shall call upon me, and I will answer him: I (will be) with him in trouble; I will deliver him, and honour him.

Psalms 91:14, 15

Be strong and of a good courage, fear not, nor be afraid of them: for the LORD thy God, he (it is) that doth go with thee; he will not fail thee, nor forsake thee.

Deuteronomy 31:6

Why art thou cast down, O my soul? and why art thou disquieted within me? hope in God: for I shall yet praise him, (who is) the health of my countenance, and my God.

Psalms 43:5

If my people, which are called by my named, shall humble themselves, and pray, and seek my face, and turn from their wicked ways; then will I hear from heaven, and will forgive their sin, and will heal their land.

II Chronicles 7:14

So Moses brought Israel from the Red sea, and they went out into the wilderness of Shur; and they went three days in the wilderness, and found no water.

And when they came to Marah, they could not drink of the waters of Marah, for they (were) bitter: therefore the name of it was called Marah.

And the people murmured against Moses, saying, What shall we drink?

And he cried unto the LORD; and the LORD shewed him a tree, (which) when he had cast into the waters, the waters were made sweet: there he made for them a statute and an ordinance, and there he proved them,

And said, If thou wilt diligently hearken to the voice of the LORD thy God, and wilt do that which is right in his sight, and wilt give ear to his commandments, and keep all his statutes, I will put none of these diseases upon thee, which I have brought upon the Egyptians: for I (am) the LORD that healeth thee.

Exodus 15:22-26

(A Song of degrees.) I will lift up mine eyes unto the hills, from whence cometh my help.

My help (cometh) from the LORD, which made heaven and earth.

Psalms 121:1, 2

Casting all your care upon him; for he careth for you.

I Peter 5:7

When thou passest through the waters, I (will be) with thee; and through the rivers, they shall not overflow thee: when thou walkest through the fire, thou shalt not be burned; neither shall the flame kindle upon thee.

Isaiah 43:2

He giveth power to the faint; and to (them that have) no might he increaseth strength.

Even the youths shall faint and be weary, and the young men shall utterly fall:

But they that wait upon the LORD shall renew (their) strength; they shall mount up with wings as eagles; they shall run, and not be weary; (and) they shall walk, and not faint.

Isaiah 40:29-31

(Let your) conversation (be) without covetousness; (and be) content with such things as ye have: for he hath said, I will never leave thee, nor forsake thee.

So that we may boldly say, The Lord (is) my helper, and I will not fear what man shall do unto me.

Hebrews 13:5, 6

Let not your heart be troubled: ye believe in God, believe also in me.

John 14:1

Dealing With Business Failure

And we know that all things work together for good to them that love God, to them who are the called according to (his) purpose.

Romans 8:28

For I am persuaded, that neither death, nor life, nor angels, nor principalities, nor powers, nor things present, nor things to come,

Nor height, nor depth, nor any other creature, shall be able to separate us from the love of God, which is in Christ Jesus our Lord.

Romans 8:38, 39

For the which cause I also suffer these things: nevertheless I am not ashamed: for I know whom I have believed, and am persuaded that he is able to keep that which I have committed unto him against that day.

Hold fast the form of sound words, which thou hast heard of me, in faith and love which is in Christ Jesus.

II Timothy 1:12, 13

(It is) better to trust in the LORD than to put confidence in man.

Psalms 118:8

Therefore, brethren, stand fast, and hold the traditions which ye have been taught, whether by word, or our epistle.

Now our Lord Jesus Christ himself, and God, even our Father, which hath loved us, and hath given (us) everlasting consolation and good hope through grace,

Comfort your hearts, and stablish you in every good word and work.

II Thessalonians 2:15-17

But the Lord is faithful, who shall stablish you, and keep (you) from evil.

And we have confidence in the Lord touching you, that ye both do and will do the things which we command you.

And the Lord direct your hearts into the love of God, and into the patient waiting for Christ.

II Thessalonians 3:3-5

Strengthen ye the weak hands, and confirm the feeble knees.

Say to them (that are) of a fearful heart, Be strong, fear not: behold, your God will come (with) vengeance, (even) God (with) a recompence; he will come and save you.

Then the eyes of the blind shall be opened, and the ears of the deaf shall be unstopped.

Then shall the lame (man) leap as an hart, and the tongue of the dumb sing: for in the wilderness shall waters break out, and streams in the desert.

Isaiah 35:3-6

Fear thou not; for I (am) with thee: be not dismayed; for I (am) thy God: I will strengthen thee; yea, I will help thee; yea, I will uphold thee with the right hand of my righteousness.

Isaiah 41:10

(Maschil of David; A Prayer when he was in the cave.) I cried unto the LORD with my voice; with my voice unto the LORD did I make my supplication.

I poured out my complaint before him; I shewed before him my trouble.

When my spirit was overwhelmed within me, then thou knewest my path. In the way wherein I walked have they privily laid a snare for me.

I looked on (my) right hand, and beheld, but (there was) no man that would know me: refuge failed me; no man cared for my soul.

I cried unto thee, O LORD: I said, Thou (art) my refuge (and) my portion in the land of the living.

Attend unto my cry; for I am brought very low: deliver me from my persecutors; for they are stronger than I.

Bring my soul out of prison, that I may praise thy name: the righteous shall compass me about; for thou shalt deal bountifully with me.

Psalms 142:1-7

Charge them that are rich in this world, that they be not highminded, nor trust in uncertain riches, but in the living God, who giveth us richly all things to enjoy;

That they do good, that they be rich in good works, ready to distribute, willing to communicate;

Laying up in store for themselves a good foundation against the time to come, that they may lay hold on eternal life.

I Timothy 6:17-19

This poor man cried, and the LORD heard (him), and saved him out of all his troubles.

The angel of the LORD encampeth round about them that fear him, and delivereth them.

O taste and see that the LORD (is) good: belssed (is) the man (that) trusteth in him

O fear the LORD, ye his saints: for (there is) no want to them that fear him.

The young lions do lack, and suffer hunger: but they that seek the LORD shall not want any good (thing).

Psalms 34:6-10

If then God so clothe the grass, which is to day in the field, and to morrow is cast into the oven; how much more (will he clothe) you, O ye of little faith?

And seek not ye what ye shall eat, or what ye shall drink, neither be ye of doubtful mind.

For all these things do the nations of the world seek after: and your Father knoweth that ye have need of these things.

But rather seek ye the kingdom of God; and all these things shall be added unto you.

Luke 12:28-31

For the love of money is the root of all evil: which while some coveted after, they have erred from the faith, and pierced themselves through with many sorrows.

But thou, O man of God, flee these things; and follow after righteousness, godliness, faith, love, patience, meekness.

I Timothy 6:10, 11

Be ye angry, and sin not: let not the sun go down upon your wrath:

Neither give place to the devil.

Ephesians 4:26, 27

To him that overcometh will I grant to sit with me in my throne, even as I also overcame, and am set down with my Father in his throne.

Revelation 3:21

Be sober, be vigilant; because your adversary the devil, as a roaring lion, walketh about, seeking whom he may devour:

Whom resist stedfast in the faith, knowing that the same afflictions are accomplished in your brethren that are in the world.

But the God of all grace, who hath called us unto his eternal glory by Christ Jesus, after that ye have suffered a while, make you perfect, stablish, strengthen, settle (you).

I Peter 5:8-10

If the foundations be destroyed, what can the righteous do?

The LORD (is) in his holy temple, the LORD'S throne (is) in heaven: his eyes behold, his eyelids try, the children of men.

The LORD trieth the righteous: but the wicked and him that loveth violence his soul hateth.

Upon the wicked he shall rain snares, fire and brimstone, and an horrible tempest: (this shall be) the portion of their cup.

For the righteous LORD loveth righteousness; his countenance doth behold the upright.

Psalms 11:3-7

(We are) troubled on every side, yet not distressed; (we are) perplexed, but not in despair;

Persecuted, but not forsaken; cast down, but not destroyed;

II Corinthians 4:8, 9

For which cause we faint not; but though our outward man perish, yet the inward (man) is renewed day by day.

For our light affliction, which is but for a moment, worketh for us a far more exceeding (and) eternal weight of glory;

While we look not at the things which are seen, but at the things which are not seen: for the things which are seen (are) temporal; but the things which are not seen (are) eternal.

II Corinthians 4:16-18

Come, my people, enter thou into thy chambers, and shut thy doors about thee: hide thyself as it were for a little moment, until the indignation be overpast.

Isaiah 26:20

-255-

Problem Solving

Without counsel purposes are disappointed: but in the multitude of counsellors they are established.

Proverbs 15:22

Whoso keepeth the fig tree shall eat the fruit thereof: so he that waiteth on his master shall be honoured.

Proverbs 27:18

And he spake this parable unto them, saying,

What man of you, having an hundred sheep, if he lose one of them, doth not leave the ninety and nine in the wilderness, and go after that which is lost, until he find it?

And when he hath found (it), he layeth (it) on his shoulders, rejoicing.

And when he cometh home, he calleth together (his) friends and neighbours, saying unto them, Rejoice with me; for I have found my sheep which was lost.

Either what woman having ten pieces of silver, if she lose one piece, doth not light a candle, and sweep the house, and seek diligently till she find (it)?

And when she hath found (it), she calleth (her) friends and (her) neighbours together, saying, Rejoice with me; for I have found the piece which I had lost.

Luke 15:3-6, 8, 9

And when it was evening, his disciples came to him, saying, This is a desert place, and the time is now past; send the multitude away, that they may go into the villages, and buy themselves victuals.

But Jesus said unto them, They need not depart; give ye them to eat.

And they say unto him, We have here but five loaves, and two fishes.

He said, Bring them hither to me.

And he commanded the multitude to sit down on the grass, and took the five loaves, and the two fishes, and looking up to heaven, he blessed, and brake, and gave the loaves to (his) disciples, and the disciples to the multitude.

And they did all eat, and were filled: and they took up of the fragments that remained twelve baskets full.

Matthew 14:15-20

Then said the king, The one saith, This (is) my son that liveth, and thy son (is) the dead: and the other saith, Nay; but thy son (is) the dead, and my son (is) the living.

And the king said, Bring me a sword. And they brought a sword before the king.

And the king said, Divide the living child in two, and give half to the one, and half to the other.

Then spake the woman whose the living child (was) unto the king, for her bowels yearned upon her son, and she said, O my lord, give her the living child, and in no wise slay it. But the other said, Let it be neither mine nor thine, (but) divide (it).

Then the king answered and said, Give her the living child, and in no wise slay it: she (is) the mother thereof.

And all Israel heard of the judgment which the king had judged; and they feared the king: for they saw that the wisdom of God (was) in him, to do judgment.

I Kings 3:23-28

Two (are) better than one; because they have a good reward for their labour.

For if they fall, the one will lift up his fellow: but woe to him (that is) alone when he falleth; for (he hath) not another to help him up.

Again, if two lie together, then they have heat: but how can one be warm (alone)?

And if one prevail against him, two shall withstand him; and a threefold cord is not quickly broken.

Ecclesiastes 4:9-12

Rest & Replenishment

Come unto me, all (ye) that labour and are
heavy laden, and I will give you rest.

Take my yoke upon you, and learn of me; for
I am meek and lowly in heart: and ye shall find rest
unto your souls.

For my yoke (is) easy, and my burden is
light.

Matthew 11:28, 29

Rest in the LORD, and wait patiently for him:
fret not thyself because of him who prospereth in his
way, because of the man who bringeth wicked
devices to pass.

Psalms 37:7

Thus the heavens and the earth were finished,
and all the host of them.

And on the seventh day God ended his work
which he had made; and he rested on the seventh day
from all his work which he had made.

And God blessed the seventh day, and sanc-
tified it: because that in it he had rested from all his
work which God created and made.

Genesis 2:1-3

Six days thou shalt do thy work, and on the
seventh day thou shalt rest: that thine ox and thine ass
may rest, and the son of thy handmaid, and the
stranger, may be refreshed.

Exodus 23:12

And the LORD spake unto Moses, saying,

Speak thou also unto the children of Israel, saying, Verily my sabbaths ye shall keep: for it (is) a sign between me and you throughout your generations; that (ye) may know that I (am) the LORD that doth sanctify you.

Ye shall keep the sabbath therefore; for it (is) holy unto you: every one that defileth it shall surely be put to death: for whosoever doeth (any) work therein, that soul shall be cut off from among his people.

Six days may work be done; but in the seventh (is) the sabbath of rest, holy to the LORD: whosoever doeth (any) work in the sabbath day, he shall surely be put to death.

Wherefore the children of Israel shall keep the sabbath, to observe the sabbath throughout their generations, (for) a perpetual covenant.

It (is) a sign between me and the children of Israel for ever: for (in) six days the LORD made heaven and earth, and on the seventh day he rested, and was refreshed.

Exodus 31:12-17

And the apostles gathered themselves together unto Jesus, and told him all things, both what they had done, and what they had taught.

And he said unto them, Come ye yourselves apart into a desert place, and rest a while: for there were many coming and going, and they had no leisure so much as to eat.

And they departed into a desert place by ship privately.

Mark 6:30-32

What? know ye not that your body is the temple of the Holy Ghost (which is) in you, which ye have of God, and ye are not your own?

For ye are bought with a price: therefore glorify God in your body, and in your spirit, which are God's.

I Corinthians 6:19, 20

Then I commended mirth, because a man hath no better thing under the sun, than to eat, and to drink, and to be merry: for that shall abide with him of his labour the days of his life, which God giveth him under the sun.

Ecclesiastes 8:15

He that dwelleth in the secret place of the most High shall abide under the shadow of the Almighty.

I will say of the LORD, (He is) my refuge and my fortress: my God; in him will I trust.

Surely he shall deliver thee from the snare of the fowler, (and) from the noisome pestilence.

He shall cover thee with his feathers, and under his wings shalt thou trust: his truth (shall be thy) shield and buckler.

Thou shalt not be afraid for the terror by night; (nor) for the arrow (that) flieth by day.

(Nor) for the pestilence (that) walketh in darkness; (nor) for the destruction (that) wasteth at noonday.

For he shall give his angels charge over thee, to keep thee in all thy ways.

They shall bear thee up in (their) hands, lest thou dash thy foot against a stone.

Psalms 91:1-6, 11, 12

The LORD (is) thy keeper: the LORD (is) thy shade upon thy right hand.

The sun shall not smite thee by day, nor the moon by night.

The LORD shall preserve thee from all evil: he shall preserve thy soul.

The LORD shall preserve thy going out and thy coming in from this time forth, and even for evermore.

Psalms 121:5-8

Let us therefore fear, lest, a promise being left (us) of entering into his rest, any of you should seem to come short of it.

For unto us was the gospel preached, as well as unto them: but the word preached did not profit them, not being mixed with faith in them that heard (it).

For we which have believed do enter into rest, as he said, As I have sworn in my wrath, if they shall enter into my rest: although the works were finished from the foundation of the world.

For he spake in a certain place of the seventh (day) on this wise, And God did rest the seventh day from all his works.

And in this (place) again, If they shall enter into my rest.

Seeing therefore it remaineth that some must enter therein, and they to whom it was first preached entered not in because of unbelief:

Again, he limiteth a certain day, saying in David, To day, after so long a time; as it is said, To day if ye will hear his voice, harden not your hearts.

For if Jesus had given them rest, then would he not afterward have spoken of another day.

There remaineth therefore a rest to the people of God.

For he that is entered into his rest, he also hath ceased from his own works, as God (did) from his.

Let us labour therefore to enter into that rest, lest any man fall after the same example of unbelief.
Hebrews 4:1-11

The righteous perisheth, and no man layeth (it) to heart: and merciful men (are) taken away, none considering that the righteous is taken away from the evil (to come).

He shall enter into peace: they shall rest in their beds, (each one) walking (in) his uprightness.
Isaiah 57:1, 2

Biblical Strengths For Your Business Success...

Leadership

Lead me, O LORD, in thy righteousness because of mine enemies; make thy way straight before my face.

Psalms 5:8

Lead me in thy truth, and teach me: for thou (art) the God of my salvation; on thee do I wait all the day.

Psalms 25:5

I will instruct thee and teach thee in the way which thou shalt go: I will guide thee with mine eye.

Psalms 32:8

Trust in the LORD with all thine heart; and lean not unto thine own understanding.

In all thy ways acknowledge him, and he shall direct thy paths.

Proverbs 3:5, 6

Thus saith the LORD, thy Redeemer, the Holy One of Israel; I (am) the Lord thy God which teacheth thee to profit, which leadeth thee by the way (that) thou shouldest go.

Isaiah 58:17

And the LORD shall guide thee continually, and satisfy thy soul in drought, and make fat thy bones: and thou shalt be like a watered garden, and like a spring of water, whose waters fail not.

Isaiah 58:11

Now the LORD had said unto Abram, Get thee out of thy country, and from thy kindred, and from thy father's house, unto a land that I will shew thee:

And I will make of thee a great nation, and I will bless thee, and make thy name great; and thou shalt be a blessing:

And I will bless them that bless thee, and curse him that curseth thee: and in thee shall all families of the earth be blessed.

Genesis 12:1-3

But be ye doers of the word, and not hearers only, deceiving your own selves.

For if any be a hearer of the word, and not a doer, he is like unto a man beholding his natural face in a glass:

For he beholdeth himself, and goeth his way, and straightway forgetteth what manner of man he was.

James 1:22-24

The elders which are among you I exhort, who am also an elder, and a witness of the sufferings of Christ, and also a partaker of the glory that shall be revealed:

Feed the flock of God which is among you, taking the oversight (thereof), not by constraint, but willingly; not for filthy lucre, but of a ready mind;

Neither as being lords over (God's) heritage, but being ensamples to the flock.

And when the chief Shepherd shall appear, ye shall receive a crown of glory that fadeth not away.

I Peter 5:1-4

And Pharaoh said unto Joseph, Forasmuch as God hath shewed thee all this, (there is) none so discreet and wise as thou (art):

Thou shalt be over my house, and according unto thy word shall all my people be ruled: only in the throne will I be greater than thou.

And Pharaoh said unto Joseph, See, I have set thee over all the land of Egypt.

Genesis 41:39-41

Now we command you, brethren, in the name of our Lord Jesus Christ, that ye withdraw yourselves from every brother that walketh disorderly, and not after the tradition which he received of us.

For yourselves know how ye ought to follow us: for we behaved not ourselves disorderly among you;

Neither did we eat any man's bread for nought; but wrought with labour and travail night and day, that we might not be chargeable to any of you:

Not because we have not power, but to make ourselves an ensample unto you to follow us.

II Thessalonians 3:6-9

And I am come down to deliver them out of the hand of the Egyptians, and to bring them up out of that land unto a good land and a large, unto a land flowing with milk and honey; unto the place of the Canaanites, and the Hittites, and the Amorites, and the Perizzites, and the Hivites, and the Jebusites.

Now therefore, behold, the cry of the children of Israel is come unto me: and I have also seen the oppression wherewith the Egyptians oppress them.

Come now therefore, and I will send thee unto Pharaoh, that thou mayest bring forth my people the children of Israel out of Egypt.

Exodus 3:8-10

Now after the death of Moses the servant of the LORD it came to pass, that the LORD spake unto Joshua the son of Nun, Moses' minister, saying,

Moses my servant is dead; now therefore arise, go over this Jordan, thou, and all this people, unto the land which I do give to them, (even) to the children of Israel.

Every place that the sole of your foot shall tread upon, that have I given unto you, as I said unto Moses.

There shall not any man be able to stand before thee all the days of thy life: as I was with Moses, (so) I will be with thee: I will not fail thee, nor forsake thee.

Joshua 1:1-3, 5

And the angel of the LORD appeared unto him, and said unto him, The LORD (is) with thee, thou mighty man of valour.

And Gideon said unto him, Oh my Lord, if the LORD be with us, why then is all this befallen us? and where (be) all his miracles which our fathers told us of, saying, Did not the LORD bring us up from Egypt? but now the LORD hath forsaken us, and delivered us into the hands of the Midianites.

And the LORD looked upon him, and said, Go in this thy might, and thou shalt save Israel from the hand of the Midianites: have not I sent thee?

And he said unto him, Oh my Lord, wherewith shall I save Israel? behold, my family (is) poor in Manasseh, and I (am) the least in my father's house.

And the LORD said unto him, Surely I will be with thee, and thou shalt smite the Midianites as one man.

Judges 6:12-16

Brethren, be followers together of me, and mark them which walk so as ye have us for an ensample.

Philippians 3:17

Yet thou in thy manifold mercies forsookest them not in the wilderness: the pillar of the cloud departed not from them by day, to lead them in the way; neither the pillar of fire by night, to shew them light, and the way wherein they should go.

Nehemiah 9:19

How oft did they provoke him in the wilderness, (and) grieve him in the desert!

Yea, they turned back and tempted God, and limited the Holy One of Israel.

But made his own people to go forth like sheep, and guided them in the wilderness like a flock.

And he led them on safely, so that they feared not: but the sea overwhelmed their enemies.

Psalms 78:40, 41, 52, 53

And the LORD went before them by day in a pillar of a cloud, to lead them the way; and by night in a pillar of fire, to give them light; to go by day and night:

Exodus 13:21

Now therefore, I pray thee, if I have found grace in thy sight, shew me now thy way, that I may know thee, that I may find grace in thy sight: and consider that this nation (is) thy people.

Exodus 33:13

To him the porter openeth; and the sheep hear his voice: and he calleth his own sheep by name, and leadeth them out.

And when he putteth forth his own sheep, he goeth before them, and the sheep follow him: for they know his voice.

Then said Jesus unto them again, Verily, verily, I say unto you, I am the door of the sheep.

All that ever came before me are thieves and robbers: but the sheep did not hear them.

I am the door: by me if any man enter in, he shall be saved, and shall go in and out, and find pasture.

The thief cometh not, but for to steal, and to kill, and to destroy: I am come that they might have life, and that they might have (it) more abundantly.

I am the good shepherd: the good shepherd giveth his life for the sheep.

John 10:3, 4, 7-11

Communication

Let the words of my mouth, and the meditation of my heart, be acceptable in thy sight, O LORD, my strength, and my redeemer.

Psalms 19:14

Again, ye have heard that it hath been said by them of old time, Thou shalt not forswear thyself, but shalt perform unto the Lord thine oaths:

But I say unto you, Swear not at all; neither by heaven; for it is God's throne:

Nor by the earth; for it is his footstool: neither by Jerusalem; for it is the city of the great King.

Neither shalt thou swear by thy head, because thou canst not make one hair white or black.

But let your communication be, Yea, yea; Nay, nay: for whatsoever is more than these cometh of evil.

Matthew 5:33-37

Let no corrupt communication proceed out of your mouth, but that which is good to the use of edifying, that it may minister grace unto the hearers.

And grieve not the Holy Spirit of God, whereby ye are sealed unto the day of redemption.

Let all bitterness, and wrath, and anger, and clamour, and evil speaking, be put away from you, with all malice:

And be ye kind one to another, tenderhearted, forgiving one another, even as God for Christ's sake hath forgiven you.

Ephesians 4:29-32

My brethren, be not many masters, knowing that we shall receive the greater condemnation.

For in many things we offend all. If any man offend not in word, the same (is) a perfect man, (and) able also to bridle the whole body.

Behold, we put bits in the horses' mouths, that they may obey us; and we turn about their whole body.

Behold also the ships, which though (they be) so great, and (are) driven of fierce winds, yet are they turned about with a very small helm, withersoever the govenor listeth.

Even so the tongue is a little member, and boasteth great things. Behold, how great a matter a little fire kindleth!

And the tongue (is) a fire, a world of iniquity: so is the tongue among our members, that it defileth the whole body, and setteth on fire the course of nature; and it is set on fire of hell.

For every kind of beasts, and of birds, and of serpents, and of things in the sea, is tamed, and hath been tamed of mankind:

But the tongue can no man tame; (it is) an unruly evil, full of deadly poison.

Therewith bless we God, even the Father; and therewith curse we men, which are made after the similitude of God.

Out of the same mouth proceedeth blessing and cursing. My brethren, these things ought not so to be.

Can the fig tree, my brethren, bear olive berries? either a vine, figs? so (can) no fountain both yield salt water and fresh.

Who (is) a wise man and endued with knowledge among you? let him shew out of a good conversation his works with meekness of wisdom.

James 3:1-10, 12, 13

Do not err, my beloved brethren.

James 1:16

He that keepeth his mouth keepeth his life: (but) he that openeth wide his lips shall have destruction.

Proverbs 13:3

But as he which hath called you is holy, so be ye holy in all manner of conversation;

I Peter 1:15

He that hath knowledge spareth his words: (and) a man of understanding is of an excellent spirit.

Even a fool, when he holdeth his peace, is counted wise: (and) he that shutteth his lips (is esteemed) a man of understanding.

Proverbs 17:27, 28

A good man out of the good treasure of his heart bringeth forth that which is good; and an evil man out of the evil treasure of his heart bringeth forth that which is evil: for of the abundance of the heart his mouth speaketh.

Luke 6:45

Let him that is taught in the word communicate unto him that teacheth in all good things.

Galatians 6:6

Who (is) a wise man and endued with knowledge among you? let him shew out of a good conversation his works with meekness of wisdom.

James 3:1-10, 12, 13

The tongue of the wise useth knowledge aright: but the mouth of fools poureth out foolishness.

Proverbs 15:2

A man hath joy by the answer of his mouth: and a word (spoken) in due season, how good (is it)!

Proverbs 15:23

Be not a witness against thy neighbour without cause; and deceive (not) with thy lips.

Proverbs 24:28

A fool's mouth (is) his destruction, and his lips (are) the snare of his soul.

Proverbs 18:7

The words of a talebearer (are) as wounds, and they go down into the innermost parts of the belly.

Proverbs 18:8

For he that will love life, and see good days, let him refrain his tongue from evil, and his lips that they speak no guile:

I Peter 3:10

The words of a man's mouth (are as) deep waters, (and) the wellspring of wisdom (as) a flowing brook.

Proverbs 18:4

Confidence

Beloved, if our heart condemn us not, (then) have we confidence toward God.

And whatsoever we ask, we receive of him, because we keep his commandments, and do those things that are pleasing in his sight.

I John 3:21, 22

(There is) therefore now no condemnation to them which are in Christ Jesus, who walk not after the flesh, but after the Spirit.

Romans 8:1

Verily, verily, I say unto you, He that believeth on me, the works that I do shall he do also; and greater (works) than these shall he do; because I go unto my Father.

And whatsoever ye shall ask in my name, that will I do, that the Father may be glorified in the Son.

If ye shall ask any thing in my name, I will do (it).

John 14:12-14

I am crucified with Christ: nevertheless I live; yet not I, but Christ liveth in me: and the life which I now live in the flesh I live by the faith of the Son of God, who loved me, and gave himself for me.

Galatians 2:20

And now, little children, abide in him; that, when he shall appear, we may have confidence, and not be ashamed before him at his coming.

I John 2:28

In the fear of the LORD (is) strong confidence: and his children shall have a place of refuge.

Proverbs 14:26

And they went and came to Moses, and to Aaron, and to all the congregation of the children of Israel, unto the wilderness of Paran, to Kadesh; and brought back word unto them, and unto all the congregation, and shewed them the fruit of the land.

And they told him, and said, We came unto the land whither thou sentest us, and surely it floweth with milk and honey; and this (is) the fruit of it.

Nevertheless the people (be) strong that dwell in the land, and the cities (are) walled, (and) very great: and moreover we saw the children of Anak there.

The Amalekites dwell in the land of the south: and the Hittites, and the Jebusites, and the Amorites, dwell in the mountains: and the Canaanites dwell by the sea, and by the coast of Jordan.

And Caleb stilled the people before Moses, and said, Let us go up at once, and possess it; for we are well able to overcome it.

But the men that went up with him said, We be not able to go up against the people; for they (are) stronger than we.

And they brought up an evil report of the land which they had searched unto the children of Israel, saying, The land, through which we have gone to search it, (is) a land that eateth up the inhabitants thereof; and all the people that we saw in it (are) men of a great stature.

And there we saw the giants, the sons of Anak, (which come) of the giants: and we were in our own sight as grasshoppers, and so we were in their sight.

Numbers 13:26-33

For thus saith the Lord GOD, the Holy One o f Israel; In returning and rest shall ye be saved; in quietness and in confidence shall be your strength: and ye would not.

Isaiah 30:15

Cast not away therefore your confidence, which hath great recompence of reward.

For ye have need of patience, that, after ye have done the will of God, ye might receive the promise.

For yet a little while, and he that shall come will come, and will not tarry.

Now the just shall live by faith: but if (any man) draw back, my soul shall have no pleasure in him.

But we are not of them who draw back unto perdition; but of them that believe to the saving of the soul.

Hebrews 10:35-39

Greater love hath no man than this, that a man lay down his life for his friends.

John 15:13

And Moses said unto the LORD, O my Lord, I (am) not eloquent, neither heretofore, nor since thou hast spoken unto thy servant: but I (am) slow of speech, and of a slow tongue.

And the LORD said unto him, Who hath made man's mouth? or who maketh the dumb, or deaf, or the seeing, or the blind? have not I the LORD?

Now therefore go, and I will be with thy mouth, and teach thee what thou shalt say.

Exodus 4:10-12

But Daniel purposed in his heart that he would not defile himself with the portion of the king's meat, nor with the wine which he drank: therefore he requested of the prince of the eunuchs that he might not defile himself.

Now God had brought Daniel into favour and tender love with the prince of the eunuchs.

And the prince of the eunuchs said unto Daniel, I fear my lord the king, who hath appointed your meat and your drink: for why should he see your faces worse liking than the children which (are) of your sort? then shall ye make (me) endanger my head to the king.

Then said Daniel to Melzar, whom the prince of the eunuchs had set over Daniel, Hananiah, Mishael, and Azariah,

Prove thy servants, I beseech thee, ten days; and let them give us pulse to eat, and water to drink.

Then let our countenances be looked upon before thee, and the countenance of the children that eat of the portion of the king's meat: and as thou seest, deal with thy servants.

So he consented to them in this matter, and proved them ten days.

And at the end of ten days their countenances appeared fairer and fatter in flesh than all the children which did eat the portion of the king's meat.

Thus Melzar took away the portion of their meat, and the wine that they should drink; and gave them pulse.

As for these four children, God gave them knowledge and skill in all learning and wisdom: and Daniel had understanding in all visions and dreams.

Now at the end of the days that the king had said he should bring them in, then the prince of the eunuchs brought them in before Nebuchadnezzar.

And the king communed with them; and among them all was found none like Daniel, Hananiah, Mishael, and Azariah: therefore stood they before the king.

And in all matters of wisdom (and) understanding, that the king inquired of them, he found them ten times better than all the magicians (and) astrologers that (were) in all his realm.

Daniel 1:8-20

Be not afraid of sudden fear, neither of the desolation of the wicked, when it cometh.

For the LORD shall be thy confidence, and shall keep thy foot from being taken.

Proverbs 3:25, 26

In the fear of the LORD (is) strong confidence: and his children shall have a place of refuge.

Proverbs 14:26

That your rejoicing may be more abundant in Jesus Christ for me by my coming to you again.

Philippians 1:26

And we know that all things work together for good to them that love God, to them who are the called according to (his) purpose.

Romans 8:28

For I am persuaded, that neither death, nor life, nor angels, nor principalities, nor powers, nor things present, nor things to come,

Nor height, nor depth, nor any other creature, shall be able to separate us from the love of God, which is in Christ Jesus our Lord.

Romans 8:38, 39

For the which cause I also suffer these things: nevertheless I am not ashamed: for I know whom I have believed, and am persuaded that he is able to keep that which I have committed unto him against that day.

II Timothy 1:12

Therefore will not we fear, though the earth be removed, and though the mountains be carried into the midst of the sea;

(Though) the waters thereof roar (and) be troubled, (though) the mountains shake with the swelling thereof. Selah.

(There is) a river, the streams whereof shall make glad the city of God, the holy (place) of the tabernacles of the most High.

God (is) in the midst of her; she shall not be moved: God shall help her, (and that) right early.

Psalms 46:2-5

Fear thou not; for I (am) with thee: be not dismayed; for I (am) thy God: I will strengthen thee; yea, I will help thee; yea, I will uphold thee with the right hand of my righteousness.

Isaiah 41:10

Be strong and courageous, be not afraid nor dismayed for the king of Assyria, nor for all the multitude that (is) with him: for (there be) more with us than with him:

With him (is) an arm of flesh; but with us (is) the LORD our God to help us, and to fight our battles. And the people rested themselves upon the words of Hezekiah king of Judah.

II Chronicles 32:7, 8

And they rose early in the morning, and went forth into the wilderness of Tekoa: and as they went forth, Jehoshaphat stood and said, Hear me, O Judah, and ye inhabitants of Jerusalem; Believe in the LORD your God, so shall ye be established; believe his prophets, so shall ye prosper.

II Chronicles 20:20

Spiritual Growth

If ye walk in my statutes, and keep my commandments, and do them;

Then I will give you rain in due season, and the land shall yield her increase, and the trees of the field shall yield their fruit.

And your threshing shall reach unto the vintage, and the vintage shall reach unto the sowing time: and ye shall eat your bread to the full, and dwell in your land safely.

Leviticus 26:3-5

But take diligent heed to do the commandment and the law, which Moses the servant of the LORD charged you, to love the LORD your God, and to walk in all his ways, and to keep his commandments, and to cleave unto him, and to serve him with all your heart and with all your soul.

Joshua 22:5

Only fear the LORD, and serve him in truth with all your heart; for consider how great (things) he hath done for you.

I Samuel 12:24

I am the true vine, and my Father is the husbandman.

Every branch in me that beareth not fruit he taketh away: and every (branch) that beareth fruit, he purgeth it, that it may bring forth more fruit.

Now ye are clean through the word which I have spoken unto you.

Abide in me, and I in you. As the branch cannot bear fruit of itself, except it abide in the vine; no more can ye, except ye abide in me.

I am the vine, ye (are) the branches: He that abideth in me, and I in him, the same bringeth forth much fruit: for without me ye can do nothing.

If a man abide not in me, he is cast forth as a branch, and is withered; and men gather them, and cast (them) into the fire, and they are burned.

If ye abide in me, and my words abide in you, ye shall ask what ye will, and it shall be done unto you.

Herein is my Father glorified, that ye bear much fruit; so shall ye be my disciples.

John 15:1-8

I beseech you therefore, brethren, by the mercies of God, that ye present your bodies a living sacrifice, holy, acceptable unto God, (which is) your reasonable service.

And be not conformed to this world: but be ye transformed by the renewing of your mind, that ye may prove what (is) that good, and acceptable, and perfect, will of God.

Romans 12:1, 2

All scripture (is) given by inspiration of God, and (is) profitable for doctrine, for reproof, for correction, for instruction in righteousness:

That the man of God may be perfect, throughly furnished unto all good works.

II Timothy 3:16, 17

As newborn babes, desire the sincere milk of the word, that ye may grow thereby:

I Peter 2:2

And the Lord make you to increase and abound in love one toward another, and toward all (men), even as we (do) toward you:

To the end he may stablish your hearts unblameable in holiness before God, even our Father, at the coming of our Lord Jesus Christ with all his saints.

I Thessalonians 3:12, 13

According as his divine power hath given unto us all things that (pertain) unto life and godliness, through the knowledge of him that hath called us to glory and virtue:

Whereby are given unto us exceeding great and precious promises: that by these ye might be partakers of the divine nature, having escaped the corruption that is in the world through lust.

And beside this, giving all diligence, add to your faith virtue; and to virtue knowledge;

And to knowledge temperance; and to temperance patience; and to patience godliness;

And to godliness brotherly kindness; and to brotherly kindness charity.

II Peter 1:3-7

But grow in grace, and (in) the knowledge of our Lord and Saviour Jesus Christ. To him (be) glory both now and for ever. Amen.

II Peter 3:18

And the child Samuel grew on, and was in favour both with the LORD, and also with men.

I Samuel 2:26

And the child grew, and waxed strong in spirit, filled with wisdom: and the grace of God was upon him.

And when they had fulfilled the days, as they returned, the child Jesus tarried behind in Jerusalem; and Joseph and his mother knew not of (it).

And it came to pass, that after three days they found him in the temple, sitting in the midst of the doctors, both hearing them, and asking them questions.

And all that heard him were astonished at his understanding and answers.

And Jesus increased in wisdom and stature, and in favour with God and man.

Luke 2:40, 43, 46, 47, 52

When I was a child, I spake as a child, I understood as a child, I thought as a child: but when I became a man, I put away childish things.

I Corinthians 13:11

Brethren, be not children in understanding: howbeit in malice be ye children, but in understanding be men.

I Corinthians 14:20

But strong meat belongeth to them that are of full age, (even) those who by reason of use have their senses exercised to discern both good and evil.

Hebrews 5:14

Let no man despise thy youth; but be thou an example of the believers, in word, in conversation, in charity, in spirit, in faith, in purity.

Till I come, give attendance to reading, to exhortation, to doctrine.

Neglect not the gift that is in thee, which was given thee by prophecy, with the laying on of the hands of the presbytery.

Meditate upon these things; give thyself wholly to them; that thy profiting may appear to all.

Take heed unto thyself, and unto the doctrine; continue in them: for in doing this thou shalt both save thyself, and them that hear thee.

I Timothy 4:12-16

The thief cometh not, but for to steal, and to kill, and to destroy: I am come that they might have life, and that they might have (it) more abundantly.

John 10:10

For this cause I bow my knees unto the Father of our Lord Jesus Christ,

Of whom the whole family in heaven and earth is named,

That he would grant you, according to the riches of his glory, to be strengthened with might by his Spirit in the inner man;

That Christ may dwell in your hearts by faith; that ye, being rooted and grounded in love,

May be able to comprehend with all saints what (is) the breadth, and length, and depth, and height;

And to know the love of Christ, which passeth knowledge, that ye might be filled with all the fulness of God.

Ephesians 3:14-19

Decision Making

What man (is) he that feareth the LORD? him
shall he teach in the way (that) he shall choose.

Psalms 25:12

I beseech you therefore, brethren, by the
mercies of God, that ye present your bodies a living
sacrifice, holy, acceptable unto God, (which is) your
reasonable service.

And be not conformed to this world: but be
ye transformed by the renewing of your mind, that
ye may prove what (is) that good, and acceptable,
and perfect, will of God.

Romans 12:1, 2

I will instruct thee and teach thee in the way
which thou shalt go: I will guide thee with mine eye.

Psalms 32:8

For it is God which worketh in you both to
will and to do of (his) good pleasure.

Philippians 2:13

Trust in the LORD with all thine heart; and
lean not unto thine own understanding.

In all thy ways acknowledge him, and he shall
direct thy paths.

Proverbs 3:5, 6

And if it seem evil unto you to serve the LORD, choose you this day whom ye will serve; whether the gods which your fathers served that (were) on the other side of the flood, or the gods of the Amorites, in whose land ye dwell: but as for me and my house, we will serve the LORD.

Joshua 24:15

For the LORD giveth wisdom: out of his mouth (cometh) knowledge and understanding.

He layeth up sound wisdom for the righteous: (he is) a buckler to them that walk uprightly.

He keepeth the paths of judgment, and preserveth the way of his saints.

Then shalt thou understand righteousness, and judgment, and equity; (yea), every good path.

Proverbs 2:6-9

For the which cause I also suffer these things: nevertheless I am not ashamed: for I know whom I have believed, and am persuaded that he is able to keep that which I have committed unto him against that day.

II Timothy 1:12

But seek ye first the kingdom of God, and his righteousness; and all these things shall be added unto you.

Matthew 6:33

Thou wilt keep (him) in perfect peace, (whose) mind (is) stayed (on thee): because he trusteth in thee.

Isaiah 26:3

He that answereth a matter before he heareth (it), it (is) folly and shame unto him.

Proverbs 18:13

Call unto me, and I will answer thee, and shew thee great and mighty things, which thou knowest not.

Jeremiah 33:3

Also, (that) the soul (be) without knowledge, (it is) not good; and he that hasteth with (his) feet sinneth.

Proverbs 19:2

Where no counsel (is), the people fall: but in the multitude of counsellors (there is) safety.

Proverbs 11:14

And Moses chose able men out of all Israel, and made them heads over the people, rulers of thousands, rulers of hundreds, rulers of fifties, and rulers of tens.

And they judged the people at all seasons: the hard causes they brought unto Moses, but every small matter they judged themselves.

Exodus 18:25, 26

One man esteemeth one day above another: another esteemeth every day (alike). Let every man be fully persuaded in his own mind.

Romans 14:5

Without counsel purposes are disappointed: but in the multitude of counsellors they are established.

Proverbs 15:22

He that hath knowledge spareth his words: (and) a man of understanding is of an excellent spirit.
Even a fool, when he holdeth his peace, is counted wise: (and) he that shutteth his lips (is esteemed) a man of understanding.

Proverbs 17:27, 28

For by wise counsel thou shalt make thy war: and in multitude of counsellors (there is) safety.

Proverbs 24:6

A double minded man (is) unstable in all his ways.

James 1:8

Let thine eyes look right on, and let thine eyelids look straight before thee.

Proverbs 4:25

Go, gather together all the Jews that are present in Shushan, and fast ye for me, and neither eat nor drink three days, night or day: I also and my maidens will fast likewise; and so will I go in unto the king, which (is) not according to the law: and if I perish, I perish.

Esther 4:16

One (thing) have I desired of the LORD, that will I seek after; that I may dwell in the house of the LORD all the days of my life, to behold the beauty of the LORD, and to inquire in his temple.

Psalms 27:4

No servant can serve two masters: for either he will hate the one, and love the other; or else he will hold to the one, and despise the other. Ye cannot serve God and mammon.

Luke 16:13

And when he came to himself, he said, How many hired servants of my father's have bread enough and to spare, and I perish with hunger!

I will arise and go to my father, and will say unto him, Father, I have sinned against heaven, and before thee,

And am no more worthy to be called thy son: make me as one of thy hired servants.

But the father said to his servants, Bring forth the best robe, and put (it) on him; and put a ring on his hand, and shoes on (his) feet:

And bring hither the fatted calf, and kill (it); and let us eat, and be merry:

For this my son was dead, and is alive again; he was lost, and is found. And they began to be merry.

Luke 15:17-19, 22-24

Motivation

And whatsoever ye do, do it heartily, as unto
the Lord, and not unto men.

Colossians 3:23

Whatsoever thy hand findeth to do, do (it)
with thy might; for (there is) no work, nor device,
nor knowledge, nor wisdom, in the grave, whither
thou goest.

Ecclesiastes 9:10

Wherefore seeing we also are compassed
about with so great a cloud of witnesses, let us lay
aside every weight, and the sin which doth so easily
beset (us), and let us run with patience the race that
is set before us,

Looking unto Jesus the author and finisher of
(our) faith; who for the joy that was set before him
endured the cross, despising the shame, and is set
down at the right hand of the throne of God.

For consider him that endured such contra-
diction of sinners against himself, lest ye be wearied
and faint in your minds.

Hebrews 12:1-3

Brethren, I count not myself to have apprehended: but (this) one thing (I do), forgetting those
things which are behind, and reaching forth unto
those things which are before,

I press toward the mark for the prize of the
high calling of God in Christ Jesus.

Philippians 3:13, 14

For it is God which worketh in you both to will and to do of (his) good pleasure.

Philippians 2:13

I can do all things through Christ which strengtheneth me.

Philippians 4:13

But my God shall supply all your need according to his riches in glory by Christ Jesus.

Philippians 4:19

Go ye therefore, and teach all nations, baptizing them in the name of the Father, and of the Son, and of the Holy Ghost:

Teaching them to observe all things whatsoever I have commanded you: and, lo, I am with you alway, (even) unto the end of the world. Amen.

Matthew 28:19, 20

But ye shall receive power, after that the Holy Ghost is come upon you: and ye shall be witnesses unto me both in Jerusalem, and in all Judaea, and in Samaria, and unto the uttermost part of the earth.

Acts 1:8

Be strong and of a good courage, fear not, nor be afraid of them: for the LORD thy God, he (it is) that doth go with thee; he will not fail thee, nor forsake thee.

Deuteronomy 31:6

Then said I unto them, Ye see the distress that we (are) in, how Jerusalem (lieth) waste, and the gates thereof are burned with fire: come, and let us build up the wall of Jerusalem, that we be no more a reproach.

Then I told them of the hand of my God which was good upon me; as also the king's words that he had spoken unto me. And they said, Let us rise up and build. So they strengthened their hands for (this) good (work).

Nehemiah 2:17, 18

Simon Peter saith unto them, I go a fishing. They say unto him, We also go with thee. They went forth, and entered into a ship immediately; and that night they caught nothing.

But when the morning was now come, Jesus stood on the shore: but the disciples knew not that it was Jesus.

Then Jesus saith unto them, Children, have ye any meat? They answered him, No.

And he said unto them, Cast the net on the right side of the ship, and ye shall find. They cast therefore, and now they were not able to draw it for the multitude of fishes.

John 21:3-6

He giveth power to the faint; and to (them that have) no might he increaseth strength.

Even the youths shall faint and be weary, and the young men shall utterly fall:

But they that wait upon the LORD shall renew (their) strength; they shall mount up with wings as eagles; they shall run, and not be weary; (and) they shall walk, and not faint.

Isaiah 40:29-31

Ye are of God, little children, and have overcome them: because greater is he that is in you, than he that is in the world.

I John 4:4

And whatsoever ye shall ask in my name, that will I do, that the Father may be glorified in the Son.

If ye shall ask any thing in my name, I will do (it).

John 14:13, 14

Know ye not that they which run in a race run all, but one receiveth the prize? So run, that ye may obtain.

And every man that striveth for the mastery is temperate in all things. Now they (do it) to obtain a corruptible crown; but we an incorruptible.

I therefore so run, not as uncertainly; so fight I, not as one that beateth the air:

But I keep under my body, and bring (it) into subjection: lest that by any means, when I have preached to others, I myself should be a castaway.

I Corinthians 9:24-27

And seek not ye what ye shall eat, or what ye shall drink, neither be ye of doubtful mind.

For all these things do the nations of the world seek after: and your Father knoweth that ye have need of these things.

But rather seek ye the kingdom of God; and all these things shall be added unto you.

Luke 12:29-31

For even when we were with you, this we commanded you, that if any would not work, neither should he eat.

For we hear that there are some which walk among you disorderly, working not at all, but are busybodies.

Now them that are such we command and exhort by our Lord Jesus Christ, that with quietness they work, and eat their own bread.

But ye, brethren, be not weary in well doing.

II Thessalonians 3:10-13

The thoughts of the diligent (tend) only to plenteousness; but of every one (that is) hasty only to want.

Proverbs 21:5

PERSONAL STUDY NOTES

_____
_____
_____
_____
_____
_____
_____
_____
_____
_____
_____
_____
_____
_____
_____
_____
_____
_____
_____
_____
_____
_____
_____
_____
_____
_____
_____
_____

PERSONAL STUDY NOTES

_____
_____
_____
_____
_____
_____
_____
_____
_____
_____
_____
_____
_____
_____
_____
_____
_____
_____
_____
_____
_____
_____
_____
_____
_____
_____
_____
_____
_____

PERSONAL STUDY NOTES

_____
_____
_____
_____
_____
_____
_____
_____
_____
_____
_____
_____
_____
_____
_____
_____
_____
_____
_____
_____
_____
_____
_____
_____
_____
_____
_____
_____
_____
_____
_____
_____

PERSONAL STUDY NOTES

_____
_____
_____
_____
_____
_____
_____
_____
_____
_____
_____
_____
_____
_____
_____
_____
_____
_____
_____
_____
_____
_____
_____
_____
_____
_____
_____
_____

PERSONAL STUDY NOTES

_____

_____

_____

_____

_____

_____

_____

_____

_____

_____

_____

_____

_____

_____

_____

_____

_____

_____

_____

_____

_____

_____

_____

_____

_____

_____

_____

_____

PERSONAL STUDY NOTES

Printed in the USA
CPSIA information can be obtained
at www.ICGtesting.com
JSHW032052190324
59504JS00010B/70